STARLIGHT SPECIALS

STARLIGHT SPECIALS

The Overnight Anglo-Scottish Express

DAVE PEEL

AMBERLEY

Above: 6011 *Enterprise* on the 9.40 p.m. ex-EW (Sat). Seen on Sunday 3 May 1953, crossing the 4-tracked LMR plus DC and underground lines north of Wembley Central. (Brian Holyland)
Front cover: See page 19. (J. L. Stevenson) *Back cover*: Here a tram stops outside Glasgow Central station in 1956, and one of the last Glasgow Fair Starlights is seen at Shield's Road in July 1962. (*Left*: W. D. McMillar/J. L. Stevenson Collection. *Right*: W. A. C. Smith/Transport Treasury)

First published 2014

Amberley Publishing
The Hill, Stroud
Gloucestershire, GL5 4EP

www.amberley-books.com

British Library Cataloguing in Publication Data.
A catalogue record for this book is available from the British Library.

ISBN 978 1 4456 4142 3 (print)
ISBN 978 1 4456 4174 4 (ebook)

Typeset in 10pt on 12pt Sabon.
Typesetting and Origination by Amberley Publishing.
Printed in the UK.

Contents

Acknowledgements

This book could not have been prepared without the assistance of the following, to whom grateful thanks are offered.

The National Archive, Kew; the National Railway Museum; Manchester Locomotive Society; Great Central Railway Society; the National Archive of Scotland; Modern Railways; the Scottish Railway Preservation Society; British Railways Board (Residuary); the 'Head of Steam' Museum (Darlington); Armstrong Railway Photographic Trust; the Transport Treasury; Railway Correspondence & Travel Society; Transport Ticket Society; John Macnab; Hamish Stevenson; Brian Pask; Brian Holyland; Brian Morrison; Sam Woods; Tommy Knox; David Kingman; Chris Coates; John Chamney; David Holmes; John Marsh; Simon Fowler.

While every effort has been made to ensure that the photographic attributions are accurate, if this is not the case the author would welcome contact from the true copyright holder.

Preface

At first sight this book seems to be yet another about the titled Anglo-Scottish expresses of the 1950s and 1960s, and it is true that these trains were introduced, ran, and were also withdrawn, on dates that correspond (within a month or two) to the entire service period of the famous King's Cross–Edinburgh 'Elizabethan'. Like this train, Starlights were powered by A4s (sometimes, for sections of the journey) and 11-coach rakes of selected stock were also the norm, all in the latest BR livery, and refreshment facilities were provided. They were even, like the 'Elizabethan', non-stop between London and Edinburgh so far as passengers were concerned (though stops for engine and crew changes were made en route), and in addition Starlights mainly operated during the currency of the summer timetable only.

Here, however, all correspondence ends! Starlight Specials were, as their name suggests, overnight trains, but without sleeping cars. They did not run daily, but only departed on Friday nights and returned on Saturday nights, and were not advertised in the public timetable! They were, in fact, all holiday excursion trains, running as demand required, passengers booking (in advance) to return eight or fifteen days later. If demand did not warrant the running of an excursion train, it did not run. At the other extreme, when demand was high, Starlights ran in multiple portions, with as many as ten to twelve trains departing the same terminal in one night. The attractiveness of these trains lay in the cheap fares, designed to combat road competition, as the specials were one-class only (third, later second, class). These were never 'express' trains, with schedules of ten plus hours for the 400 or so miles, and, again unlike the 'Elizabethan', did not run from King's Cross.

Those Starlights running to Edinburgh (Waverley) commenced at Marylebone (an unusual station for traffic to Scotland) and ran via the GC main line to the Sheffield area, then across to York to join the east coast route northwards. However, the bulk of the Starlight Specials did not use this route at all but travelled (also non-stop) between St Pancras and Glasgow (St Enoch) via Leeds and Carlisle. Indeed, the overall majority of passengers were Glaswegians heading south, and this traffic was the backbone of the service throughout the entire period of operations.

Here then is an account of these trains, their successes and failures, their rise and their fall, over the ten-year period that they made a profit for BR. Much of the information contained here is from 'management' sources held at the National Archive at Kew, and provides an insight into some of the difficulties in putting on such a flexible service. It must be remembered that this involved the Scottish, Eastern and London Midland regions (and, to a lesser extent the North-Eastern region as well) in jointly operating 400-mile excursions on a regular (though not publically timetabled) basis, sometimes with twenty-plus trains running over a peak weekend on two already busy routes. This was no easy task, and these were not 'ordinary' excursion trains.

Introduction

The Commercial Case

During 1952, British Railways began drawing up plans to combat the growing long-distance Anglo-Scottish road-coach traffic. Not the daily, daytime services so much as the holiday traffic, much of which travelled overnight in both directions and was seen to be vulnerable to transfer to rail if a suitably attractive alternative could be offered.

At this time, the Scottish Omnibuses Ltd overnight express carriage fare was 60s return between Edinburgh and London, while the Glasgow-based private operator Northern Roadways – who claimed to offer special amenities such as an on-board toilet, and included a breakfast – was charging 75s return (on the same route) and had begun this alternative service in 1951. This firm had also obtained a licence for a Glasgow–London overnight service in competition with the nationalised Western Scottish Omnibuses Ltd. These two state-owned companies were therefore in direct competition with Northern Roadways on both the Glasgow–London and Edinburgh–London routes.

Early in 1953, BR therefore began taking advance bookings for a new overnight excursion service to run between St Pancras and Glasgow (St Enoch) and between Marylebone and Edinburgh (Waverley) and vice versa. These trains would only operate from Easter to September and would offer departures on Friday nights, with return journeys on Saturday nights eight or fifteen days hence. These were therefore 'period' returns but priced most attractively at 70s return, instead of the usual third-class return fare of 114s 8d between Waverley and Marylebone and 117s 4d between St Enoch and St Pancras. The cheap fare also included the 1s seat reservation fee, and an all-night cafeteria car service was to be available, which also served breakfasts at 3s 6d. Accommodation (third class only) was to be in modern compartment stock (either late LMS or late LNER designs), three-a-side with armrests – the type considered the most appropriate for long-distance overnight travel. Children aged three to thirteen would be carried at half-fare. As far as passengers were concerned, these trains would be non-stop, with no opportunity to alight or board at any intermediate station, though as can be seen from the schedules these were not 'quick' trains. In 1953 the overnight England to Scotland road journeys were taking some fifteen and a half hours; the proposed overnight rail schedules were ten and a half or less.

As a package, this was an imaginative effort by BR both to beat the road competition and to hopefully generate new rail traffic between these main centres. Given that the round trip covered roughly 800 miles, the fare worked out at approximately 1*d* per mile and this was immediately seen as good value. The trains were marketed under the title Starlight Specials and this branding was also applied to the rolling stock, there being four sets of carriage roof boards on each side of the eleven-coach sets that made up the standard formation.

Easter 1953, therefore, saw the commencement of one of BR's most successful Anglo-Scottish overnight services, especially popular from Glasgow (the ScR were largely responsible for the initiative), and one which was to last for no fewer than ten years. The initial format did change somewhat over subsequent seasons, but at no time were these trains advertised in the public timetables, all being excursions run on demand, all publicity being local to the terminal stations, selected 'feeder' stations and in press releases.

The Service Provided

As advertised, the timings were to be as follows:

Friday nights (outward departure)

London (St Pancras) dep. 11.0 p.m.   London (Marylebone) dep. 10.5 p.m.
Glasgow (St Enoch) arr. 9.35 a.m.   Edinburgh (Waverley) arr. 7.42 a.m. *

Glasgow (St Enoch) dep. 8.25 p.m.   Edinburgh (Waverley) dep. 9.40 p.m.
London (St Pancras) arr. 6.50 a.m.   London (Marylebone) arr. 6.50 a.m.

Saturday nights (return journeys)

St Pancras dep. 10.40 p.m.   Marylebone dep. 10.5 p.m.
St Enoch arr. 8.45 a.m.   Waverley arr. 7.42 a.m. *

St Enoch dep. 8.25 p.m.   Waverley dep. 9.40 p.m.
St Pancras arr. 6.50 a.m.   Marylebone arr. 6.50 a.m.

* 7.59 a.m. in summer timetable

* * *

Thirty years after the demise of the Great Central, 'Marylebone for Scotland' at long last became a reality.

The above timings applied only to the 'parent' train; if bookings warranted two or more specials, these duplicates clearly had different schedules. The number of 'extras' was limited both by the available paths and by the rolling stock position, which could be critical at busy holiday periods. In all cases pre-booking was essential.

The Railway executive laid down that cafeteria cars (which were in short supply and in great demand for other services) must be supplied for the 'parent' train on each route, plus the first duplicate if this ran. Subsequent duplicates had to 'make do' by using the non-passenger space in a brake third corridor (BTK) coach from which to serve whatever refreshments were possible. This BTK was to occupy the same central position within the train formation as the cafeteria car (CC).

It was also laid down that a standard Starlight Special train set should consist of eleven vehicles as follows: BTK/4TK/CC/4TK/BTK (where TK was the third corridor, weighing 345 tons (LMS stock) or 363 tons (LNER stock)). Additionally, all stock was to be in the latest carmine and cream livery.

The maximum possible formation on the Marylebone route was eleven vehicles, while twelve was possible on the St Pancras route. If demand was low, a reduced formation could be employed on either route, though strengthened to twelve on the St Pancras route if this was warranted.

The route taken by trains running between St Pancras and St Enoch was that of the old Midland Railway to Leeds (through Leicester, Trent, Sheffield and Rotherham), thence to Skipton, followed by the Settle & Carlisle line. Beyond that, specials took the ex-G&SWR route through Kilmarnock to reach St Enoch. Engines were changed once, at Leeds Whitehall Junction without reversal.

The route taken between Marylebone and Waverley was an innovation, however. This was via the GC main line (either High Wycombe or Aylesbury) to Leicester and Nottingham as far as Darnall on the outskirts of Sheffield, then Swinton, Church Fenton and York. After this, the east coast main line was followed to Newcastle and finally Edinburgh. Perhaps surprisingly, engines were changed three times, at Leicester, York and Newcastle.

Rolling stock was provided by the Scottish Region for specials originating at Edinburgh/Glasgow, by the Eastern Region for specials from Marylebone, and by the London Midland Region for specials from St Pancras (there was an exception for Glasgow Fair traffic, which will be discussed later).

Coaching stock was serviced at either Bellahouston Carriage Sidings (for Glasgow Traffic) or Craigentinny CS (for Edinburgh trains). In London, Starlights using St Pancras were serviced at Cricklewood CS or, for Marylebone trains, at Neasden CS. Post-war LMS stock had seven compartments providing forty-two seats per TK, plus four compartments (twenty-four seats) in the BTK's at each end, making a total of 384 seats per eleven-coach train. Pre-war LNER coaches provided forty-eight seats per TK (eight compartments) plus a further thirty-six seats in each BTK, making a maximum capacity of 456 passengers per eleven-coach set. The cafeteria cars did not 'match' the uniformity of the other stock very well, being largely a hotch-potch of conversions from ex-GE or GN dining cars (including twelve-wheeled vehicles) or pre-war Gresley catering stock.

In addition to a guard and cafeteria car staff, a travelling ticket collector was provided on each Starlight, who also acted as a courier.

Southbound passengers travelling to London (or beyond) but connecting with a Starlight at St Enoch or Waverley via a local service simply booked ordinary return fare from their home town to Glasgow or Edinburgh as an add-on to their Starlight fare. They booked similarly beyond London if this was appropriate, and of course in the northbound direction also. (In subsequent years, some specials began back at other Scottish towns or cities to eliminate the connection, though the add-on fare still applied.)

STARTING 10th APRIL 1953

★ GLASGOW ~~117'4d~~

★ EDINBURGH ~~114'8d~~

BY
"STARLIGHT
SPECIAL"
THIRD CLASS ONLY

ONLY
70'-
RAIL RETURN

CHILDREN
THREE YEARS
AND UNDER
FOURTEEN YEARS
35'-

★ LONDON

★ STAY 8 OR 15 DAYS
★ EXPRESS OVERNIGHT TRAVEL
★ RESERVED SEATS
★ NIGHT BUFFET
★ ADVANCE BOOKINGS ESSENTIAL

★ "STARLIGHT SPECIAL" TRAINS are a new facility offered to the public by British Railways. On Fridays from 10th April to 18th September inclusive, the special trains will run between London and Edinburgh and London and Glasgow and passengers will return by special trains on Saturday nights the 8th or 15th day after arrival. The tickets are only available by the special trains shown overleaf and on the dates shown on the tickets.

★ "STARLIGHT SPECIAL" TRAINS offer a reserved seat to all passengers travelling by the service. Accommodation is limited and for this reason it is ESSENTIAL that passengers BOOK IN ADVANCE stating the date on which they desire to travel forward and return.

★ "STARLIGHT SPECIAL" TRAINS are available ONLY to holders of "Starlight Special" tickets specifying the appropriate train and date of travel.

P.T.O.

BRITISH RAILWAYS

★ "STARLIGHT SPECIAL" TRAINS run as shown below, and light refreshments are obtainable on them in both directions.

OUTWARD JOURNEY — FRIDAY NIGHTS

London St. Pancras dep. 11.0 p.m.	London Mary'ne dep. 10.5 p.m.
Glasgow St. Enoch arr. 9.35 a.m.	Edinburgh Wav. arr. *7.42 a.m.

*—arrives 7.59 a.m. on and from 13th June.

RETURN JOURNEY — SATURDAY NIGHTS

Glasgow St. Enoch dep. 8.25 p.m.	Edinburgh Wav. dep. 9.40 p.m.
London St. Pancras arr. 6.50 a.m.	London Mary'ne arr. 6.50 a.m.

★ "STARLIGHT SPECIAL" TRAIN tickets are on sale at London Terminal Stations and Town Offices, also at principal suburban stations and Railway Ticket Agents in the London Area. Postal applications should be directed to:—

For bookings to Edinburgh —Enquiry Office, Marylebone Station, London N.W.1.

For bookings to Glasgow —Enquiry Office, St. Pancras Station, London N.W.1.

Combined travel and reservation tickets are only obtainable on payment at time of booking.

★ "STARLIGHT SPECIAL" TICKETS ARE NOT TRANSFERABLE and are issued subject to the Bye-Laws, Regulations and Conditions contained in the Publications and Notices of or applicable to the Railway Executive. They are not available for break of journey. The Railway Executive do not undertake to refund the value of lost, mislaid or unused tickets. Further information may be obtained on application to stations or agencies or to

FOR TRAVEL TO GLASGOW	FOR TRAVEL TO EDINBURGH
W. N. Roberts	N. H. Briant
District Passenger Superintendent	District Operating Superintendent
Euston Station	Paddington Station
London N.W.1	London W.2

Travel light—send your luggage in advance

For passengers who prefer a Combined Road/Rail facility to Scotland by ordinary services (out by road, return by rail or vice versa) tickets are obtainable at a fare of 80/- from Scottish Omnibuses Ltd., 298 Regent Street, London W.1, who will supply details on request

Printed by W. A. SMITH (Leeds) LTD.   B.R. 35001

(BRB Residuary)

The 1953 Season

By mid-March, over 15,000 bookings had been made and all six trains for the outward Glasgow Fair traffic from St Enoch on Friday 17 July were completely sold out. By 8 April over 20,000 advanced bookings had already been received, including 1,100 seats in the four trains to be run on the inaugural night.

In the Beginning

Friday 10 April: Down Trains

Marylebone dep. 10.50 p.m. behind A3 60111 *Enterprise* as far as Leicester
          then behind A3 60048 *Doncaster* to York
          then behind A1 60142 *Edward Fletcher* to Newcastle
          then behind A4 60011 *Empire of India* to Edinburgh
St Pancras dep. 11.0 p.m. behind 'Jubilee' 45627 *Sierra Leone* to Leeds
          then behind 'Royal Scot' 46133 *The Green Howards* to Glasgow

Up Trains

Waverley dep. 9.40 p.m. behind A4 60011 *Empire of India* as far as Newcastle
          then behind A1 60142 *Edward Fletcher* to York
          then behind V2 60963 to Leicester
          then behind A3 60111 *Enterprise* to Marylebone
St Enoch dep. 8.25 p.m. behind 2P 40621 + 'Jubilee' 45665 *Lord Rutherford of Nelson*
          then behind 'Jubilee' 45573 *Newfoundland* from Leeds

All four were 'parent' trains on their outward journeys (returns not being possible for eight days at least) and all were equipped with cafeteria cars, the 8.25 p.m. from St Enoch having one of LNER origin. It will be appreciated that in the absence of returning trains these unbalanced workings gave rise to long-distance empty stock movements (see 'Repercussions').

Friday 10 April. The inaugural Starlight Special from Marylebone was headed, most appropriately, by 60111 *Enterprise* (34E Neasden) and this loco worked all the Friday and Saturday departures from Marylebone, and the return workings from Leicester, until 10 May inclusive with the exception of the weekend of 24/25 April when 60051 *Blink Bonny* was in charge. (Brian Morrison)

Although the Up trains departed Waverley and St Enoch at their advertised Friday times, the Marylebone departure used the Saturday timing and the St Pancras train utilised one of the conditional paths, rather than 10.40 p.m. as indicated on the handbill. Note also that this handbill was intended for traffic originating in London as it does not give outward journey times from Scotland.

Generally speaking, the Marylebone–Waverley route excursions were powered by Pacifics or V2s, occasionally supplemented by B1s. Leicester engines were infrequent visitors to York other than on Starlights, though once there were often used on 'fill-in' turns to Newcastle and back prior to taking a southbound Starlight if there was one.

Although not a passenger stop, Down trains changing engines at Newcastle were run into platforms 8, 9 or 10 in order to supply water to the cafeteria car. Up trains had a similar servicing stop at Leicester (Central).

On the St Pancras–St Enoch route, motive power was usually either a 'Royal Scot' or a 'Jubilee', backed up by Stanier 'Black 5s'. Southbound departures from St Enoch would commonly be piloted by a 2P 4-4-0 as far as New Cumnock. Leeds (Holbeck) engines

Platform scene at St Enoch: happy Glaswegians prior to departure. Note the style of roof-board – inverted commas and no definite article in the title. (British Railways)

were also unusual arrivals into St Enoch, as these were normally changed at Carlisle when on service trains. The same was true for Corkerhill locos reaching Leeds.

Up trains would also make a servicing stop at either Nottingham (Midland) or Leicester (London Road) to take on extra water for the catering vehicle, especially if this was a BTK and not a full cafeteria car. Down trains did this at Carlisle.

* * *

In the early part of the season, holiday bookings were such that only one train set was required on each route, this working both the Friday outward and Saturday return excursions. However, as the summer progressed, further sets had to be introduced to meet demand. The Eastern Region provided four sets:

Set no. 1 introduced on Friday 10 April through to Friday 18 September.
Set no. 2 introduced on Friday 19 June* through to Saturday 5 September.

Both formations being BTK/4TK/CC/4TK/BTK with eleven vehicles.

Set no. 3 began on Friday 26 June (not used every week); BTK/8TK/BTK
Set no. 4 began on Friday 3 July (not used every week); BTK/9TK/BTK

* on Saturday 13 June a second set was required and an ex-LMS set was supplied by the LMR, headed by a B1 out of Marylebone.

Thus the ER supplied forty-three vehicles (maximum), plus two extra ScR sets, for Marylebone–Waverley workings at the busiest times. In the case of sets 3 and 4, refreshments were served from BTKs at the ends of each set, in contravention of the 'laid down' formation.

Hence, on Friday 3 July, six Starlight Specials departed Marylebone (the maximum number of paths available), five running via High Wycombe, one via Harrow, including two sets of ex-LMS stock provided by the ScR.

On the LM route on the same weekend – Friday 3/Saturday 4 July – seven Starlights ran from St Enoch to St Pancras plus two (of twelve coaches each) to Euston, carrying, in total, 3,695 passengers. Two Starlights also ran northbound so that, overall, twenty-seven specials ran, carrying 9,624 passengers.

The following weekend – Friday 10/Saturday 11 July – saw a further twenty Starlights running, conveying 6,567 passengers.

Friday 17 July was the busiest, however, taking outbound Glasgow Fair holiday traffic, so that twelve Starlights left St Enoch, seven for St Pancras and five for Euston, plus four in the reverse direction – employing no less than 188 corridor coaches in total. (Timings for some of these appear in the accompanying Special Traffic Notices extract).

The grand total for this weekend – 17/18 July – therefore amounted to forty-five Starlights (both routes) carrying approximately 17,000 passengers.

To set this Glasgow Fair traffic in context, it is illuminating to recall the extent to which the Scottish Region was able to lay on a *very* extensive programme of excursions at this time, as the following extract from the *BR Magazine* for September 1953 reveals:

With 200 special trains at the service of Glasgow holidaymakers for the rush to the coast and country, we (*the Scottish Region*) certainly played no mean part in freeing the folks at the 'Fair'.

The 'holiday bargain' for the year attracted an exodus of no less than 5,000 to London by Starlight Specials on the evening of Friday July 17, when the Starlight ran in twelve portions from St Enoch, with neither fuss, temper or tears – so well was it organised.

The spotlight can also be turned on the through train from Buchanan Street direct to Dover, where 500 passengers embarked for Ostend.

A further eight relief trains to London were arranged for Friday 17 and Saturday 18 July, and over thirty specials ran to Blackpool, Manchester and the Midlands of England as well as York and Scarborough.

Twenty-eight trains in addition to the normal programme served Aberdeen, Inverness, Wick, and Thurso districts, while twenty-five special trains went to Edinburgh and the Fife Coast.

Many extra trains took the sailing contingent via Stranraer and Ardrossan to Ireland and the Isle of Man, and via Fairlie, Wemyss Bay and Gourock to the Clyde coast.

Friday 5 June. 40621 and 45711 *Courageous* power the neat rake of LMS stock in carmine and cream livery forming the 8 p.m. parent train out of St Enoch past Crossmyloof. Note Corkerhill's unique combined 'headboard plus train reporting number' displayed on the pilot engine. (J. L. Stevenson)

Friday 3 July. 45491 heads the 7.15 p.m. relief (M592) from St Enoch through Bellahouston. (J. L. Stevenson)

Congestion has occurred at Glasgow stations in past years during the fair because of passengers who, though reserving seats, crowded the stations an hour or more before the departure times of their trains. The publicity given to this had its effect this year and there was a marked diminution of unnecessary queuing at all stations.

A fortnight later, the Bank Holiday weekend – Friday 31 July/Saturday 1 August – saw seven Starlights from St Enoch to St Pancras plus one to Euston (carrying 3,351 passengers), two Starlights from Paisley to St Pancras, and four Starlights from St Pancras to St Enoch.

After these weekends demand gradually subsided, the last outward departure being on Friday 18 September, the last return being made on Saturday 3 October.

Observations of train workings throughout the season

April/May, 45687 *Neptune* (67A Corkerhill) generally works all St Enoch to St Pancras Starlights as far as Leeds, with pilot 40621 (usually) to New Cumnock.

10 April–June, of the nineteen Starlights worked to or from Marylebone, 60111 *Enterprise* works ten trains, 60051 *Blink Bonny* works two trains, and 61001 *Eland* works four trains, all either to or from Leicester.

18/25 April, 45573 *Newfoundland* works all Up Leeds–St Pancras trains

2/9/16 May, 45573 *Newfoundland* works all Down St Pancras–Leeds Starlights.

Friday 15 May, 45648 *Wemyss* heads 11.0 p.m. from St Pancras to Leeds.

Friday 5 June, 40621 and 45711 *Courageous* on M4 at Crossmyloof.

Friday 3 July, 45491 on M592 (7.15 p.m. from St Enoch), Bellahouston.

Saturday 4 July, 61001 *Eland* at Sudbury & Harrow Road on the 9.40 p.m. from Waverley.

Friday 17 July, 44821 on same train as 45491, again at Bellahouston.

Further details of the five trains to Euston from St Enoch, all of which stop at Crewe to pick up refreshments. Formation: BTK/4TK/CC?/5TK/BTK with twelve coaches of 375 tons:

> W528 arrives at Euston at 4.20 a.m.
> W529 arrives at Euston at 5.15 a.m.
> W530 arrives at Euston at 5.38 a.m.
> W531 arrives at Euston at 7.30 a.m.
> W532 arrives at Euston at 7.55 a.m.

Friday 31 July, 60543 *Irish Elegance* heads 9.50 p.m. from Waverley to York, and 60529 *Pearl Diver* heads 9.20 p.m. from Waverley to York.

Saturday 5 September, 60049 *Galtee More* works Down Starlight Leicester–York.

Sunday 6 September, 60049 seen on Up parcels, Newcastle–York, fill-in turn.

Saturday 3 October, 61163 heads last Down Starlight, Marylebone–Leicester.

Sunday 4 October, 61163 returns from Leicester with last Up train.

Saturday 4 July. 61001 *Eland* runs through Sudbury & Harrow Road station at 7.19 a.m. on the 9.40 p.m. from Waverley (Friday). Note the 'Starlight Special' roof-board on the leading Gresley BSK. This engine shared most of these workings during the early summer with 60111. (Brian Holyland)

Friday 17 July. 44821 this time heads the 7.15 p.m. relief, again through Bellahouston. This train was due into St Pancras at 5.58 a.m – see the extract from the Special Traffic Notices. (J. L. Stevenson)

Coaching stock. Inaugural train from Marylebone comprised of post-war LNER coaches plus twelve-wheeled cafeteria car E43043E. First train out of St Enoch probably had one of the cafeteria cars SC670E – SC673E in its formation. On 13 June the duplicate from Marylebone to Waverley was composed entirely of ex-LMS stock.

Financial Results	Receipts (£)	Costs (£)	Net profit (£)
St Pancras/Glasgow	51,937	20,851	31,086
Marylebone/Edinburgh	47,801	21,429	26,372
Glasgow/St Pancras	89,207	30,995	58,212
Edinburgh/Marylebone	61,732	24,908	36,824
Totals	250,677	98,183	152,494

From this net profit an allowance was made in respect of refunds on unused tickets of approximately £10,000. However, regard must also be paid to any savings accruing as a result of reliefs to ordinary trains not being required, which would otherwise have run, without the introduction of the Starlight facility.

Repercussions from the 1953 season

As hinted at above, on busy summer weekends when multiple Starlights were in operation great pressure was created on the rolling stock departments. Many other excursions were also booked on each weekend in summer and demand for good-quality modern compartment stock was intense; additionally, cafeteria cars were also in short supply.

Even on the 'quieter' east coast route, provision of stock for Starlights caused a relief train from Peterborough to Newcastle on 30 July to be cancelled, a relief train from King's Cross to Edinburgh and from King's Cross to Newcastle on 31 July to be cancelled, and one from Sheffield to Norwich on 1 August to also be cancelled.

Plus, throughout the period of Starlight operation, the ER instigated quicker turnaround of stock, leading to reduced cleaning and servicing times; reduction of train set formations, leading to overcrowding; failure to provide strengthening stock (either rostered or casual) for scheduled services; and replacement of corridor by non-corridor stock in some timetabled formations (indicated by *), either wholly or in part. Additionally, there were several instances of long-distance empty stock workings, as detailed in the following chart.

ECS workings of Starlight sets owing to unbalanced working of loaded sets

From	To	Stock	Remarks
Marylebone	Edinburgh	ScR	No.1 ScR set off Up train on Friday 10 April (a)
Edinburgh	Marylebone	ER	No.1 ER set off Down train on Friday 10 April (a)
Marylebone	Edinburgh	ScR	Off Up working on Friday 3 July (b)
Marylebone	Edinburgh	ScR	Off Up working on Friday 3 July (b)
Newcastle	Edinburgh	ScR	Off Up working on Friday 3 July (c)
Newcastle	Edinburgh	ScR	Off Up working on Friday 3 July (c)
Edinburgh	Marylebone	ER	Off Down working on Friday 17 July
Edinburgh	Marylebone	ER	Off Down working on Friday 17 July
Edinburgh	Marylebone	ER	Off Down working on Friday 24 July
Edinburgh	Marylebone	ER	Off Down working on Saturday 1 August
Edinburgh	Marylebone	ScR	To meet Down requirements Saturday 8 August
Edinburgh	Marylebone	ScR	To meet Down requirements Saturday 15 August
Edinburgh	Marylebone	ScR	To meet Down requirements Saturday 22 August
Newcastle	Edinburgh	ScR	Off Up working on Saturday 12 September (d)

Notes

(a) This was necessary owing to there being no balanced working on Saturday 11 April and in order to put the sets on their proper respective weekly runs from Friday 17 April.

(b) Empty Marylebone to Leicester and Sheffield respectively for local use during the weekend, then sent empty to Edinburgh.

(c) Empty sets transferred to King's Cross to work relief trains to Newcastle on the Saturday and Sunday (4th and 5th) and afterwards sent forward empty from Newcastle to Edinburgh.

(d) Empty set transferred to King's Cross to work 8.10 p.m. relief to Newcastle on Friday 18 September. Then sent forward empty from Newcastle to Edinburgh.

As the ScR/LMR ran by far the greatest number of Starlights, the effect on their rolling stock position in the peak summer period was more pronounced:

July 3/4	14 trains were subject to (*)
July 10/11	12 were subject to (*)
July 18	4 relief trains from St Pancras cancelled
	29 trains subject to (*)
July 24/25	16 trains cancelled due to shortage of rolling stock
	46 trains subject to (*)
July 31/Aug 1	38 trains cancelled
	31 trains subject to (*)
Aug 7/8	16 trains cancelled
	29 trains subject to (*)
Aug 14/15	17 trains subject to (*)

It must be noted, however, that although the rolling stock position was aggravated by the running of Starlight Specials, these were not the sole cause of the above difficulties.

At the season's end, the ER put in a strong plea for a change to train formations on the Marylebone–Waverley route excursions. Apparently, numerous complaints had been received regarding long-distance expresses from King's Cross being composed, at least partly, of 'open' stock (centre corridor, eight bays, sixty-four seats), whereas the regular formation of 'corridor' stock (seven compartments, forty-two seats) was more comfortable. (Which is why, of course, that compartment stock was laid down for overnight Starlight trains in the first place.) However, it was also argued that those paying full fare should not be travelling in less comfortable arrangements than those enjoying reduced fare tickets. This aspect was pushed forcefully, and it was also stated that, as 'open' stock carried more passengers, fewer Starlights needed to be run. The ER therefore proposed to run eleven-coach formations in 1954 consisting of BTK/4TO/CC/4TO/BTK, maximum 560 seats (eight coaches of sixty-four seats and two coaches of twenty-four seats), in comparison to 1953's arrangement of BTK/4TK/CC/4TK/BTK, maximum 384 seats (eight coaches of forty-two seats and two coaches of twenty-four seats).

This 'open' stock argument did not find favour with either the ScR or the LMR authorities, who were content with 'compartment' provision. Indeed, it was equally strongly argued by these regions that to substitute 'open' stock would be a breach of trust in respect of publicity and public expectations, especially after a successful initial operating season.

It was further suggested by the ER that similar Starlight services might be considered between other pairs of destinations, and that the London to Glasgow/Edinburgh trains be extended to Christmas/New Year operation for 1954/5. The possibility was also raised of running a combined Glasgow/Edinburgh train through to St Pancras in each direction at the beginning, and towards the end, of the season.

Another aspect of rolling stock provision that demanded much management attention after the close of the 1953 season was to limit, in some way, the sheer number of Starlights to be offered at peak times. Not only was the availability of coaching and catering stock a problem in itself, but pathing difficulties also restricted the number of trains that could be run on busy summer weekends. It also had to be taken into account that the Marylebone route could only accommodate eleven-coach formations, whereas St Pancras could accommodate twelve, Euston fourteen, and, if necessary, King's Cross fourteen also.

FRIDAY, 29th MAY.

250. PRIVATE EXCURSION.
379. ADDITIONAL TRAIN: "STARLIGHT SPECIAL."
AA. 10.0 p.m. MARYLEBONE TO MANCHESTER—RETIMED.

Class	250 A (a.m.)	250 A (p.m.)
Pleasley	7 50	
Skegby	7 55	
Sutton-in-Ashfield Town	8 0	
Kirkby South Junction	8 6	
Bagthorpe Junction	8 18	
New Basford		
Nottingham Victoria	8 w23	
,,	8 27	
Leicester Central	9 w0	
,,	9 0·5	
Woodford Halse	9 47	
Culworth Junction	9 49	
Grendon Underwood Junc.	10 9	
Ashendon Junction	10 22	
Princes Risborough	10 35	
High Wycombe	10 46	
Northolt Junction East	11 4	
Neasden Sidings		6†30
Neasden South Junction	11 13	6 32
Marylebone	11 22	6†45

Class	250 C (a.m.)	250 A (p.m.)	379 A (p.m.)	AA A (p.m.)
Marylebone	11†35	7 15	10 5	
Neasden South Junction	11 47	7 25	10 15	
Neasden North Junction	11 49			
,,	11 52			
Neasden Sidings ,,	11†55			
Northolt Junction East			10 24	
High Wycombe			10 45	
Princes Risborough			10 55	
Ashendon Junction			11 5	
Harrow		7 30		
Watford South Junction		7 45		
Rickmansworth		7 47		
Chalfont & Latimer		7 56		
Great Missenden		8 5		As bkd.
Aylesbury		8 21		*0:—
Quainton Road		8 27		
Grendon Underwood Junc.		8 30	11 15	11 19 B5
Brackley				11 40
Culworth Junction		8 51	11 36	11 51
Woodford Halse				11 55
,,		8 53	11 38	11 57
Rugby Central				12 16
,,			B3	12 21
Leicester Central		9 w33	12 17	fwd.
,,		9 38	12 23	3 mins. later
Nottingham Victoria		10 9		to:—
,,		10 A13	12 50	
New Basford				
Bagthorpe Junction		10 18	12 54	
Kirkby South Junction		10 36	1 9	
Sutton-in-Ashfield Junc.		10n43		
Skegby		10n49		
Pleasley		10 54		
Heath			1 23	
Staveley Central			1 31	
Woodhouse East Junction			1 39	2 37 B3
Darnall			1 v49	
,,			1 v55	
Sheffield Victoria				2 47
,,				3 2
Attercliffe Junction			2 0	as bkd.
Rotherham Central			2 8	
Mexborough No. 3			2 16	
Mexborough West Junc.			2 22	
York			3L14	
Edinburgh			7 42	

A.—10.15 p.m. Nottingham Victoria to Pinxton to run 3 minutes later than booked.

For Stock and Formation see next page.

An extract from Special Traffic Notices valid on Saturday 30 and Friday 29 May 1953. (BRB Residuary)

SATURDAY, 30th MAY.

446, 448. ADDITIONAL TRAINS: "STARLIGHT SPECIALS."
264, 266, 524. PARTY SPECIALS.
263. DAY EXCURSION.
AA 6.0 a.m. NOTTINGHAM TO MARYLEBONE RETIMED.

	446	448	263	264	AA	524	266
Class	A	A	A	B	B	A	A
	a.m.	a.m.	a.m.	a.m.	a.m.	a.m.	a.m.
Mexborough West Junction	2 10	2 27					
Mexborough No. 3	2 14	2 31					
Rotherham Central	2 24	2 41					
Attercliffe Junction	2 34	2 51					
Darnall	2 38	2 55					
"	2 44	3 1					
Woodhouse East Junction	2 51	3 8					
Staveley Central	2 59	3 16					
Heath	3 10	3 27			From West Hallam (dep. 6.55 a.m.).		
Kirkby-in-Ashfield Central							7 20
Kirkby South Junction	3 24	3 41					7 25
Hucknall Central							7 32
Bulwell Common							7 39
Bagthorpe Junction	3 33	3 50				7 22	7 42
Nottingham Victoria						7 27	7 47
	3 37	3 54				7 32	7 52
Loughborough Central			6 8				8H13
Quorn & W.	B1	B3	6 14				
Leicester Central	4 8	4 25	6 26				8 26
	4 15	4 32	6 31	7 35		8 2	8 31
Whetstone			6 41				
Lutterworth			6 58		As		
Rugby Central			7 8		bkd.	8 27	
			7 10		to:—	8 32	
Charwelton					8 12		
					8 22		
Charwelton Up Loop	From Edinburgh (dep. 9.20 p.m. 29th).	From Edinburgh (dep. 9.40 p.m. 29th).		8 19			
Woodford Halse					8 27		
					8 33		
	4 56	5 13	7 29	8 23	8 33	8 51	9 17
Culworth Junction	4 59	5 16	7 31	8 25		8 53	9 16
Culworth					8 40		
Helmdon					8 48		
Brackley				7 43	8 55		
Finmere					9 4		
Calvert				B	9 14		
Grendon U. Junction	5 17 B3	5 34 B6	7 56	8 46	9 17	9 28	9 39
Ashendon Junction	5 27	5 47	8 6				
Princes Risborough	5 38	5 58	8 18				
High Wycombe	5 49	6 9	8 30				
Northolt Junction E.	6 10	6 30	8 54				
Quainton Road				8 49	9 22	9 38	9 44
Aylesbury					9 32		
"				8 56 B	9 38 as	9 48	9 52
Great Missenden				9F13	bkd.	10 2	10 8
Chalfont & L.				9 25		10 14	10 21
Rickmansworth				9 32		10 20	10 28
Watford South Junction				9 34		10 22	10 30
Harrow				9 48		10 35	10 44
Neasden South Junction	6 19 B3	6 39 B3	9 5	9 55		10 41	10 49
Marylebone	6 30	6A50	9 16	10 7		10 52	11 0

A.—5.1 a.m. Parcels Aylesbury to Marylebone to arrive Marylebone 6.54 a.m.   F.—9.15 a.m. Great Missenden to Marylebone to run 8 minutes later than booked.   H.—Up Loop 7.38 a.m. Nottingham Victoria to Rugby Central to depart Loughborough Central 8.17 a.m. and run 8 minutes later forward.

For Stock, etc., see page 18.

5

SATURDAY, 18th JULY — DERBY TO ST. PANCRAS

UP

Station	A — Relief M685	A — Relief from Clitheroe C854	A — 6.30 pm (Fri) Special from Glasgow M591	A — Relief M757	A — 7.15 pm (Fri) Special from Glasgow M592	A — Relief M758	A — 7.55 pm (Fri) Special from Glasgow M593	A — 8.25 pm (Fri) Glasgow returned 4	A — 8.55 pm (Fri) from Glasgow M594	A — 8.55 pm (Fri) Glasgow St. E. to Kettering returned 8	A — 9.5 pm (Fri) from Glasgow St. E. 10	A — 9.23 pm (Fri) Special Glasgow M595
	am	am	am	am	am	am	am	am	am	am	am	am
Chaddesden C.S. ...dep	12†25											
Derby Jn.	12 33											
DERBY MIDLAND arr	12†35	1W58									5 0	
dep	12 50	2W 3									5 7	
London Road Jn.	12 51	2 4									5 8	
Sawley Jn.	1 2	2 15									5 19	
Sheet Stores Jn.	1 3	2 16									5 20	
Trent .... arr					3 15		3 51		4 49	5 3		5 28
.......dep										5 5		
Long Eaton Jn.												
Beeston												
NOTTINGHAM MIDLAND arr			2W40									
MIDLAND dep			2K50									
Melton Jn.			3 15									
Melton Mowbray			3 16									
Saxby												
Manton			3 34									
Hathern	1 10	2 23			3 22		3 58		4 56	5 12	5 27	5 35
Loughboro' Mid. arr	1 14											
dep	1 16	2 26			3 25		4 1		4 59	5 15	5 30	5 39
LEICESTER LON. RD. arr	1 33	2W44			3K41		4K16		5K15	5 30	5 46	5K58
LON. RD. dep	1 38	2W49			3K53		4K26		5K22	5 35	5 53	6K 4
Market Harboro' arr									5 43	5 56	6 15	6 27
dep	2 0	3 12			4 16		4 49		5 51	6 4	6 23	6 35
Desboro' & Rothwell	2 8	3 21			4 25		4 57					
Kettering North Jn.										6 11	6 30	
KETTERING ...... arr	2 17											
......dep	2 20	3 28	3 57 / 3X59 FL		4 32		5 3		5 57		6 32	6 41
Kettering Jn.												
Wellingboro' Mid. Rd. arr	2 29				4 40		5 10		6 3		6 40	6 49
dep	2 32	3 35	4 6				5 19		6 10		6 49	6 59
Sharnbrook Summit	2 43	3 44	4 16		4 50		5 26		6 17		6 56	7 6
Oakley	2 50 SL	3 51	4 23		4 58							
Oakley Jn.												
Bedford Mid. Rd. arr	2 54		SL									
dep	3 14	3 54	4 26	4†10½ GL	5 1		5 30		6 20		6 59	7 9
Millbrook				4 28 GL								
Harlington				4X48 FL								
Leagrave arr				4†57 FL								
dep				5 2								
LUTON MID. RD. arr	3 45											
dep	3 48	4 20	4 52	5 12	5 25	5 32	5 59	6 8	6 46		7 35	7 42
Harpenden Jn.				-5X20								
Harpenden Cen.				SL								
St. Albans City arr												
dep	4 1	4 34	5 8	5 29	5 36	5 45	6 18	6 25	6 58		7 50	7 58
Napsbury												
Mill Hill Broadway												
Hendon	4 15	4 49	5 22	5 51	5 49	6 0	6 34	6 41	7 12		8 5	8 16
Welsh Harp Jn.												
Cricklewood												
Finchley Road				5X57 FL								
Carlton Road Jn.												
Kentish Town arr												
dep	4 24	4 56	5 29	6 1	5 55	6 10	6 41	6 49	7 18		8 12	8 24
ST. PANCRAS .... arr	4 27	5 0	5 32	6 5	5 58	6 14	6 45	6 52	7 21		8 15	8 27
.....dep	5†35 ML	5†20 ML	ML	6†22 ML	6†28 ML		7†10 ML		7†47 ML			8†55 ML
St. Pancras Jn.				6X24 GL	6X30 GL		7X12 GL		7X49 GL			8X57 GL
Kentish Town	5 40	5 26	6 10	6†34								
Cattle Docks arr												
Finchley Road	5X45	5X32	6X16									
West Hampstead												
	LL	LL	LL						8X 9 FL			FL
Watling Street					6X56 FL		7X47 FL		8X12			9X22 FL
Cricklewood C.S. arr	5†53	5†40			7† 0		7†51					
Cricklewood Jn.												9X26 LL
Brent L.W.S. ....arr			6†25						8†20			9†30

Note: columns M591, M757, M592, M758, M593, M594 and train 10 are marked "LIMITED LOAD"; M591, M592, M593, train 4 and M595 are "STARLIGHT" Trains; train 4 "As booked to—".

M592. M593. M594. M595—K—To take up fresh Tea and Supplies.
M685—LE to work:—Derby E.S.S. dep 11|35 pm GL, Derby Jn. 11X37, Chaddesden C.S. arr 11|45 pm (Fri).
M758—5.50 am "B" St. Albans to St. Pancras to start from SL platform and run FL at St. Albans South.
M594—6.25 am "B" Bedford to St. Pancras to run SL to Millbrook and follow.
M595—12.25 am "C" Leeds to Bedford to follow from Kettering Jn.

Extracts from Special Traffic Notices valid from Saturday 18 July to Friday 24 July 1953. Page 5 – see columns headed M591/2/3/4/5; train 4 is also a 'Starlight'. Page 34 – see columns headed M581/3/4/5/6/7. (BRB Residuary)

34

SUNDAY, 19th JULY

LEEDS TO CARLISLE

DOWN	A 8.50 pm (Sat.) Special St. Pancras to Glasgow	A 11.15 pm (Sat.) Special St. Pancras to Glasgow	A 11.25 pm (Sat.) Special St. Pancras to Glasgow	A 11.35 pm (Sat.) Special St. Pancras to Glasgow	A 12.0 (night) Special St. Pancras to Glasgow	C 12.15 am Special St. Pancras to Glasgow	C ECS	A ECS to Barnoldswick	A Halifax to Blackpool Cen.	A Halifax to Bridlington	A Halifax to Saltburn	A Halifax	A Scenic Halifax to Whitby and Scarborough
	M581	M583	M584	M585	M586	M587	M548	—	M933	M872	916	M544	917
	v	v	v	v	v	v							
LEEDS CITY NTH. arr	am ..	am ..	am ..	am ..	am ..	am ..	am ..	am ..	am ..	am ..	am	7†30	am ..
dep	..	..	..	..	..	..	..	..	..	..	..	10 15	..
Leeds City South..dep	..	..	..	..	..	..	..	..	..	..			..
Leeds City Jn...........	..	..	..	..	..	..	..	..	..	..		SL	..
Leeds Whitehall Jn. arr	1L50	4L12	4L30	4L47	5L 5	5L52	..	..	..	..			..
dep	2* 0	4*22	4*40	4*57	5*15	6* 2	..	..	..	..			..
Wortley Jn.............	SL	SL	SL	SL	SL	SL	..	..	..	..			..
Armley Canal Road.....	..	..	..	..	..	..	..	..	..	..		10 20	..
Kirkstall.............	..	..	..	..	..	..	..	..	..	..		10 25	..
Newlay & H...........	..	..	..	..	..	..	..	..	..	..		10 30	..
Calverley & R........	..	..	..	..	..	..	..	..	..	..		10 33	..
Apperley Jn..........	..	..	..	..	..	..	..	..	..	..			..
Apperley Bridge & R.....	..	..	..	..	..	..	..	..	..	..		10 40	..
Guiseley Jn...........	..	..	..	..	..	..	..	..	..	..			..
Shipley Leeds Jn........	2 25	4 36	4 54	5 11	5 29	6 16	..	..	..	..		10 48	..
BRADFORD F.S. dep	..	..	..	..	..	..	..	..	..	..	9 50		10 53
Manningham...........	..	..	..	..	..	..	..	..					
Manningham C.S. dep	..	..	..	..	..	..	..	..	8† 5 GL	9†15 GL			
Frizinghall............	..	..	..	..	..	..	..	..					
Shipley .... arr	..	..	..	..	..	..	..	..			9 56		10 59
........dep							..	..	8 15	9 25	9 58		11 1
Manningham C.S. arr	LIMITED LOAD "STARLIGHT" Special	"STARLIGHT" Special	"STARLIGHT" Special	"STARLIGHT" Special	"STARLIGHT" Special	"STARLIGHT" Special	..	..					
Manningham...........							..	..					
BRADFORD F.S. arr							..	..					
Guiseley ......arr							..	..	9†35	10 8			11 10
......dep							..	T—Connection from Barnoldswick arrives 9.37 am	9 45	10 9			11 11
Menston ......arr							..		9 50	10 14			11 16
Otley ....arr							..		9 56	10 22			11 22
........dep							..		9 58	10 24			11 24
Ilkley...............							..						
Bolton Abbey							..						
Saltaire	..	..	..	..	..	..	..						
Bingley	..	..	..	..	..	..	..		N.E. Region P. and G.	N.E. Region C. P. and G.			N.E. Region Z.J.P. and G.
Keighley ......arr	..	..	..	..	..	..	..						
......dep	2 38	4 45	5 3	5 20	5 38	6 25	..	8 28				11 2	
Steeton & S..........	..	..	..	..	..	..	..						
Kildwick & C..........	..	..	..	..	..	..	..						
Cononley	..	..	..	..	..	..	..						
Snaygill	..	..	..	..	..	..	..						
Skipton South Jn..... arr	..	..	..	..	..	..	..						
......dep							..						
SKIPTON ....arr			5W15		5W50		..	9† 0	8†45				
........dep	2 51	4 56	5W20	5 31	5W55	6 36	..		9 30			11 16	
Thornton-in-C.	..	..	..	..	..	..			9†40				
Earby .... arr	..	..	..	..	..	..	To work 6.30 am Relief to Leeds	9 13	9 45				
............dep	..	..	..	..	..	..			9 52				
Foulridge	..	..	..	..	..	..			9 58				
Colne .... arr	..	..	..	..	..	..			10 0				
............dep													
HELLIFIELD ......arr	3W 6	5W12		5W47		6W52	For other times, see page 40		Blackpool Cen. arr 11.40 am	Bridlington arr 12.41 pm		11W37	
........dep	3W11	5W17		5W52		6W57						11W42	
Settle Jn.	3 16	5 22	5 36	5 57	6 11	7 2	..					11 49	
Clapham	..	..	..	..	..	..						12 2	
Wennington	..	..	..	..	..	..						12 13	
Lancaster G.A........	..	..	..	..	..	..						12 29	
MORECAMBE P. arr	..	..	..	..	..	..						12 37	
dep	..	..	..	..	..	..	5†30						
Heysham ....arr	..	..	..	..	..	..	5†40						
Blea Moor.............	3 38	5 47	6 5	6 22	6 40	7 27	..						
Ais Gill...............	3 51	6 1	6 19	6 36	6 54	7 41	..						
Appleby West..........	4 8	6 19	6 37	6 54	7 12	7 59	..						
CARLISLE ....arr	4 46	6 57	7 15	7 32	7 50	8 37	..						

M584—4.45 am Parcels Bradford to Carlisle to follow from Shipley Bingley Jn.

1954 Pre-Season Arrangements

After much management debate (which put back the commencement of advance bookings for 1954 until 1 February despite the road competition taking bookings pre-New Year) the following was finally resolved.

On the St Pancras–St Enoch route provision was to be made for the following:

Compartment stock to continue in use: BTK/5TK/CC/4TK/BTK of 426 seats
Maximum of four Starlight Specials (SS) run on any one night except on the following dates:

Friday 2 July   7 SS (8 actual) St Enoch–St Pancras, 12 coaches (426 seats)
        3 SS (3 actual) St Enoch–Euston, 14 coaches (510 seats)

Friday 16 July   6 SS (7 actual) St Enoch–St Pancras, 12 coaches (426 seats)
        4 SS (3 actual) St Enoch–Euston, 14 coaches (510 seats)*

* 2 sets of 'open' stock provided by the LMR, and return working 31 July (664 seats)

Friday 30 July   5 SS (6 actual) St Enoch–St Pancras, 12 coaches
        2 SS (3 actual) St Enoch–Euston, 14 coaches
        2 SS Paisley – St Pancras (did not run)

Friday 13 Aug   6 SS (4 actual) St Enoch–St Pancras

On the Marylebone–Waverley route stock provided by the ER:

Train sets to be of 'open' (centre corridor) stock.
'Parent' and first duplicate to be provided with cafeteria car (as 1953).

1st/2nd sets   BTK/4TO/CC/4TO/BTK of eleven coaches, 560 seats
3rd/4th sets   BTK/9TO/BTK of 624 seats (nine coaches of sixty-four seats and
        two coaches of twenty-four seats) with catering from end BTKs

Maximum of 2 SS outside summer timetable
Maximum of 4 SS during summer timetable with the following exceptions:

Friday 2 July   provision made for 7 SS (6 actual)
Friday 16 July   provision made for 6 SS (6 actual)
Friday 23 July   provision made for 7 SS (4 actual)
Friday 30 July   provision made for 6 SS (4 actual)

with coaching stock in excess of 4 sets provided by the LMR (LMS open stock)

On the Waverley–Marylebone route stock provided by the ScR.

Train formations to be BTK/4TK/CC/4TK/BTK of eleven coaches, 384 seats for 'parent' and first duplicate. However, in order to avoid invidious comparisons with the trains originating from Marylebone, the ScR decided to fall into line with the ER and provide open stock for Starlights originating in Edinburgh. This was despite the view of both the commercial and operating departments of the ScR that such a move was to be deprecated (for night travel), a view also shared by the Western Region commercial department, and indeed the chief of commercial services.

In all cases above and particularly at off-peak periods, train formations to be reduced according to requirements.

Easter arrangements

Departures from London commence on Maundy Thursday, 15 April (extending the eight- or fifteen-day facility to nine or sixteen days). Departures from Glasgow/ Edinburgh commence Good Friday, 16 April. The two proposals that Starlights run between Christmas and New Year, and that operation between different destinations might be worthwhile considering, were both rejected. Also, the possibility of running combined trains when demand was low was viewed with favour if suitable circumstances arose.

★ STARLIGHT SPECIAL TRAINS, one class only, will run on Friday, 9th April, Thursday 15th April, thereafter every Friday from 23rd April to 24th September inclusive, from London to Glasgow and London to Edinburgh. Passengers will return by Special trains on Saturday nights the 8th or 15th day after arrival (the 9th or 16th day in the case of passengers departing on 15th April).

★ STARLIGHT SPECIAL TRAINS assure seats to all passengers. Accommodation is limited and for this reason it is **essential** that passengers *BOOK IN ADVANCE STATING THE DATE ON WHICH THEY DESIRE TO TRAVEL FORWARD AND RETURN.*

★ STARLIGHT SPECIAL TRAINS are available **only** to holders of Starlight Special tickets specifying the appropriate train and date of travel.

★ STARLIGHT SPECIAL TRAINS run as shown below, and light refreshments are obtainable.

OUTWARD JOURNEY		RETURN JOURNEY	
FRIDAY NIGHTS		**SATURDAY NIGHTS**	
9th April to 24th September inclusive (except Good Friday, 16th April) also on Thursday, 15th April		*17th April to 9th October inclusive*	
London St. Pancras	dep. 11.00 p.m.	Glasgow St. Enoch	dep. 8.35 p.m.
Glasgow St. Enoch	arr. 9.35 a.m.	London St. Pancras	arr. 7.12 a.m.
London Marylebone	dep. 9.45 p.m.	Edinburgh Waverley	dep. 9.40 p.m.
Edinburgh Waverley	arr. 6.57 a.m.	London Marylebone	arr. 6.50 a.m.*

*7.15 a.m. from 20th June to 19th September inclusive

★ STARLIGHT SPECIAL TRAIN TICKETS, which assure a seat, are on sale at London Terminal Stations, also at principal suburban stations, Railway Ticket Offices and Ticket Agencies in the London area. Remittances for the fare, 70/- (half fare for children aged 3 but under 14 years) must accompany all postal applications to:

FOR BOOKINGS TO GLASGOW:
Enquiry Office, St. Pancras Station, London, N.W.1.

FOR BOOKINGS TO EDINBURGH:
Enquiry Office, Marylebone Station, London, N.W.1.

★ STARLIGHT SPECIAL TICKETS ARE NOT TRANSFERABLE and are issued subject to the bye-laws, regulations and conditions contained in the publications and notices of or applicable to the British Transport Commission. They are not available for break of journey. British Railways do not undertake to refund the value of lost, mislaid or unused tickets. Further information may be obtained on application to:

DISTRICT PASSENGER SUPERINTENDENT, *Euston Station, London, N.W.1*

DISTRICT OPERATING SUPERINTENDENT, *Paddington Station, London, W.2*

TRAVEL LIGHT — SEND YOUR LUGGAGE IN ADVANCE

For Passengers who prefer a Combined Road/Rail facility to Glasgow or Edinburgh by ordinary services (out by road, return by rail or vice versa) tickets are obtainable at a fare of 80/- from Scottish Omnibuses Ltd., 298, Regent Street, London, W.1, who will supply details on request.

B.R. 35001

BRITISH RAILWAYS

(BRB Residuary)

The 1954 Season

Agreed timings for this year's 'parent' trains to be as follows.

For journeys originating in Scotland:

Outward
St Enoch to St Pancras

Return
St Pancras to St Enoch

Fridays 9 April to 24 September
St Enoch dep. 8.35 p.m.
St Pancras arr. 7.12 a.m. (Saturday)

Saturday 17 April to 9 October
St Pancras dep. 10.40 p.m.
St Enoch arr. 8.45 a.m. (Sunday)
from 23/5
Central arr. 8.45 a.m. (Sunday) up to 16/5

Outward
Waverley to Marylebone
(dates as above)

Return
Marylebone to Waverley
(dates as above)

Waverley dep.   9.40 p.m.
Marylebone arr. 6.46 a.m. (Saturday); winter TT
Marylebone arr. 7.25 a.m. (Saturday); summer TT

Marylebone dep. 9.45 p.m.
Waverley arr.   7.13 a.m. (Sun)

For journeys originating in London, see handbill for timings.

Notes
Good Friday (April 16) not a Bank Holiday in Scotland.
- Running on Maundy Thursday from London eliminates some E.C S working.
- Passengers departing Maundy Thursday 15 April enjoy 9 or 16 days' holiday.
- Glasgow Central used for winter timetable arrivals from St Pancras.
- The handbill illustrated was intended for London-originating traffic only.

* * *

During the 1953 season it was considered that at least 1,000 passengers travelled to Waverley to join Starlight trains on the occasion of the Dundee, Fifeshire and Aberdeen Trades Holiday Fridays. For 1954 it was therefore decided to start the Specials back at Dundee, Kirkcaldy and Aberdeen on 9/16/23 July and to run the returning Starlights from Marylebone through to these stations also, for the convenience of this traffic.

Pre-Season Bookings

These began on 1 February (except for Glasgow Fair) and within a fortnight 3,000 tickets had been sold in Scotland alone. When Glasgow Fair bookings opened on 15 February 2,600 tickets were sold on the first day, customers arriving from 4.45 a.m. onwards for a 9 a.m. opening. Indeed, by midday on the 16th all available seats for the ten trains from St Enoch on Friday 16 July had been sold, and an estimated 1,500 additional potential passengers had to be turned away.

The Season Begins

Friday 9 April
11.0 p.m. St Pancras–St Enoch leaves behind 45612 *Jamaica* as far as Leeds and takes 46133 *The Green Howards* to Glasgow.

This twelve-coach set includes four ScR vehicles and cafeteria car M43250E, an ex-GN dining car converted at Eastleigh.

9.45 p.m. Marylebone–Waverley leaves behind 60050 *Persimmon* to Leicester. This ten-coach English set comprised nine pre-war LNER opens (all ex-works) including three with new BR upholstery, plus cafeteria car E43034E, an ex-GN twelve-wheeled dining car again converted at Eastleigh.

8.35 p.m. St Enoch–St Pancras leaves with 45665 *Lord Rutherford of Nelson* to Leeds. This nine-coach set has an ex-works engine and runs via Paisley (Gilmour St), Dalry.

9.40 p.m. Waverley–Marylebone leaves behind as far as Newcastle. This ten-coach Scottish set has nine ScR LNER opens (including one post-war steel-sided vehicle) together with cafeteria car SC671E, another Eastleigh conversion of an ex-GN dining car. (This set then formed the 9.55 p.m. King's Cross–Waverley relief on Wednesday 14 April.)

For the next seven weeks, individual bookings from the four terminal stations until the end of May are listed in the following table.

Outward Bookings From

Date	Marylebone	St Pancras	Total	Glasgow	Edinburgh	Total
Thurs 15 Apr	313	354	667			
Friday 16				420	171	591
Friday 23	139	171	310	143	107	250
Friday 30	106	123	229	197	134	331
Friday 7 May	124	155	279	197	125	322
Friday 14	182	177	359	262	179	441
Friday 21	173	232	405	282	195	477
Friday 28	300	336	636	377	211	588

Return Passengers From

Date	Marylebone	St Pancras	Total	Glasgow	Edinburgh	Total
Saturday 24 Apr	240	422	662	410	394	804
Saturday 1 May	124	220	344	254	180	434
Saturday 8	101	153	254	134	104	238
Saturday 15	121	180	301	131	103	234
Saturday 22	147	233	380	142	154	302
Saturday 29	178	272	450	233	179	412

A little later, after fourteen weeks of operation (to 9 July) it was revealed that 8 per cent more passengers had been carried in three fewer Starlights than in the equivalent period in 1953. Advance bookings at this date also showed a 10 per cent improvement from England and 23 per cent from Scotland.

The Peak Season, originating trains – outbound on Fridays

	M'bone–Edinburgh Total trains run	Edinburgh–M'bone Total trains run	St P–St Enoch Total trains run	St Enoch–St P* Total trains run
July 2	2	6		11
July 9	0	4		3
July 16	2	6	4	10
July 23	4	4	4	3
July 30	2	4	4	10
Aug 6	3	2	3	4
Aug 13	3	2	3	4

The position as regards the return services would be similar. (* and Euston)

Close to the end of the season, the LMR and ScR were able to report jointly that 15,245 passengers were conveyed or booked on the London to Glasgow service to 1 September, and that 26,643 were conveyed or booked on the Glasgow to London service to 21 August.

They also reported that the number of Starlights run, or booked to run, to the end of the season was:

London to Glasgow (London originating traffic)

Number run	Frequency		Totals
	Fridays	Saturday	
1	15	14	29
2	7	7	28
3	3	2	15
4	3	3	24
			96

Glasgow to London (Glasgow originating traffic)

1	12	12	24
2	6	2	16
4	2	2	16
5	0	1	5
10	2	2	40
11	1	1	22
			123

Notes

The maximum number of paths out of St Pancras was four.
* The extreme peak of traffic was in connection with Glasgow Fair holiday.
* On the weekend of Friday/Saturday 30/31 July the LMR cancelled nineteen trains due to no stock being available, and usual formations were reduced to the extent of 641 vehicles. Further, non-corridor stock had to be provided on fairly long-distance services to the tune of 342 coaches. As last year, the running of several Starlights aggravated the rolling stock position.
* On the vexed question of cafeteria car service versus brake van service, the LMR was able to report that, for its region, for the peak five weekends:

St Pancras–St Enoch (outward)		St Enoch–St Pancras (return)	
Friday 16 July	BTK 2 trains	Saturday 31 July	BTK 2 trains
23	2	7 Aug	2
30	2	14	2
6 Aug	1	21	1
13	1	28	1

Bearing in mind that St Pancras-originating Starlights were limited to four sets, with the 'parent' and first duplicate always having cafeteria cars, eight out of eighteen (44 per

Friday 2 July. 40605 and 45731 *Perseverance* set off from St Enoch with the Euston-bound W533. (J. L. Stevenson)

Friday 9 July. 45720 *Indomitable* is again seen at Bellahouston with M592. This station was to close on 20 September the same year. (J. L. Stevenson)

cent) of peak season traffic were having to 'make do' with sub-standard refreshment provision. This percentage was magnified in the case of Glasgow-originating passengers, where a greater proportion found themselves without a proper cafeteria car – where twenty-two seats were fitted and some socialising could take place, as opposed to the strictly 'take away' brake van facility.

Passenger preference was therefore strongly in favour of cafeteria car provision and both the LMR commercial and operating superintendents proposed (to Euston HQ) that nine LMR kitchen cars be considered for conversion to double-ended party-type cafeteria cars, the type used on the 'parent' and first duplicate trains. (Seven 'party-type' cars were indeed created at Eastleigh during 1955, though these were conversions from former ambulance train coaches, themselves originally third-class sleeping cars).

This view was reinforced by the Hotels & Catering Services whose staff bore the brunt of complaints from the public who, from the advertising literature, were led to expect a cafeteria car at all times. There was particular disappointment if the outward journey provided a cafeteria car and the return leg did not. This situation was of course similar on the Marylebone–Waverley trains, though to a rather lesser extent. (Although Hotels & Catering staff were in overall charge of the cafeteria cars, in the first year or two, 'all-night' staff were in short supply. To fill this void female volunteers from railway clerical grades were employed as 'hostesses' in dispensing drinks/snacks and clearing empties. This was especially true in the case of southbound runs from Glasgow on Fridays, and relations between 'proper' staff and the hostesses could sometimes be acrimonious. Breakages (of crockery etc.) often occurred and it was not unknown for these to be secretly deposited at speed onto the trackside and the loss blamed on passenger theft rather than be paid for out of hostesses' own pockets!)

The attraction of a quick trip to London for these 'girls' was too good to miss, and instead of availing themselves of a hostel bed (provided) before returning north the same evening, a jaunt round the sights was often preferred. Lack of sleep does, however, catch up on you, and three volunteers were prodded awake on a seat in Madam Tussauds to hear, 'Aren't they lifelike? Warm as well.')

Observations and workings throughout the season

1. Saturday 17 April, 60943 heads the English east coast set out of King's Cross as an empty stock working.
2. Friday 2 July, 40605 + 45731 *Perseverance* exit St Enoch with W533.
3. Friday 9 July, 45720 *Indomitable* heads the Up M592 at Bellahouston.
4. Friday 16 July, 41176 (61B) + 46138 *The London Irish Rifleman* (5A) take the Up W534 out of St Enoch. (61B denotes Aberdeen Ferryhill depot, though this loco was on loan to Corkerhill at the time. 5A denotes Crewe North shed. Train was bound for Euston).
5. Friday 16 July, 61116 + 61312 depart Marylebone with the 10.50 p.m., as far as Leicester.
6. Sunday 18 July, four returning Starlights seen heading north through Kilmarnock.
7. Saturday 7 Aug, 60835 *The Green Howard* powers a Starlight between Leicester and Newcastle (i.e. no engine change at York).

Further details of trains running to/from Euston are of interest, as below.

Friday 16 July	W533 ex-St Enoch	Crewe 12.53/1.0 a.m.	Euston 4.20 a.m.
	W534	1.36/1.44 a.m.	5.37 a.m.
	W535	4.12/4.19 a.m.	7.30 a.m.
	W536	4.28/4.40 a.m.	7.55 a.m.

W535 formation BTO/6TO/BTK/5TO/BTO, fourteen coaches of 420 tons
W536 has extra TO, making fifteen coaches of 450 tons

Saturday 17 July	W681 Euston 10.22 p.m.	Crewe 1.25/1.35 a.m. to St Enoch
	W701	11.5 p.m.	2.14 a.m. (non-stop)
	W703	11.55 p.m.	3.6 a.m. (n-s) to Paisley (Gil. St)

W701/3 formation BTK/5TK/BTK/6TK/BTK, fourteen coaches of 420 tons

Friday 30 July	W533 ex-Paisley (Gilmour Street)	Euston 4.24 a.m.
	W534 ex-St Enoch	Euston 5.18 a.m.
	W536 ex-St Enoch (inc. caf car)	Euston 7.55 a.m.

Saturday 31 July	W697 Euston 7.30 p.m.	Crewe 10.36/10.42 p.m. to St Enoch
	W689	9.17 p.m.	12.18 a.m. (n-s)
	W691	11.5 p.m.	2.30 a.m. (n-s)
	W695	11.55 p.m.	2.51/2.53 a.m.

All to St Enoch, and all (surprisingly, if the STN is accurate) include cafeteria cars.

Saturday 14 August W681, W701, W703 run in more or less the same times as on 17 July, but with slightly lighter loads.

Financial results for 1954 compared with 1953

	1954			1953		
Route	Receipts	Costs	Profits	Receipts	Costs	Profit
St Pancras/St Enoch	50,608	20,871	29,737	51,937	20,851	31,086
Marylebone/Edinburgh	52,598	17,131	35,467	47,801	21,429	26,372
St Enoch/St Pancras	96,054	32,199	63,855	89,207	30,995	58,212
Edinburgh/Marylebone	74,972	21,003	53,969	61,732	24,908	36,824
Totals	274,232	91,204	183,028	250,677	98,183	152,494

Deduct refunds (estimate) unused tickets	10,000	10,000
Total estimated net profit (£)	173,028	142,494

A more detailed breakdown (below) is worth examining.

	Trains Out	Trains return	Tickets adult Child	Receipts £	Loaded mileage	Costs per mile £	Train Costs £	Adv Costs £	Admin Costs £	Profit £
St P	44	45	13,366 2,187	50,608	37,979	10s 2d	19,296	1,025	550	29,737
M'ne	37	39	13,996 2,064	52,598	31,806	9s 9d	15,506	1,025	600	35,467
St E	69	72.5 *	26,196 2,496	96,054	60,563	9s 11d	30,029	1,025	1,145	63,855
Way	46	47.5 *	20,235 2,371	74,972	39,339	9s 9d	19,178	1,025	800	53,969
Totals 1954	196	204	73,793 9,118	274,232	169,667		84,009	4,100	3,095	183,028
Totals 1953	209	220	67,717 7,811	250,677	181,321		89,656	5,000	3,527	152,494

* Glasgow & Edinburgh return trains were combined on 9 October 1954

In addition to revenue from ticket sales, receipts of £13,457 accrued to the Hotels & Catering Services (Refreshment Rooms Department) in respect of the service of light refreshments on the trains.

From these financial results it will be seen that 1954 saw continued growth in the popularity of the Starlight service. The increase in profits compared with 1953 was largely made possible by the use of open stock on the east coast route, and the ER was quick to point to an increase of 16.5 per cent in their receipts and a reduction of nearly 20 per cent in their costs, whereas the West Coast services showed a 4 per cent increase in revenue and a 2 per cent increase in costs. However, the ER had to accept the fact that against these results, some 40 per cent of Scottish bookings for travel throughout the whole of the season had been made before 9 April, i.e. before passengers had had experience of travelling overnight in 'open stock' trains.

This experience resulted in many passenger criticisms of the coaches used between Marylebone and Waverley. These centred on the less comfortable two by two seating arrangement (with no separating armrests between each pair) – effectively four-a-side rather three-a-side – the inability to switch off or control lighting in any way, and the inevitable lack of separation between those walking the central aisle to go the cafeteria car (or toilet) and those trying to get some sleep.

This compartment versus open stock controversy therefore reopened with some vigour, especially in Scotland. Here, representations had been made to MPs and numerous letters of complaint had appeared in the press, with the result that the goodwill built up in 1953 for this facility had been seriously impaired. The commercial committee therefore formed the unanimous view 'that where, for commercial reasons, the Undertaking (the BTC) sets its hand to the development of business of this character, the type of stock required must be provided. If this cannot be done, it is preferable not to engage in this sort of traffic. Since this raises an issue of principle, the Committee minute it for decision accordingly'.

The use of open stock was restricted to the Marylebone–Waverley route and had initially been suggested by the ER, with the ScR later reluctantly agreeing to its use after originally proposing to repeat the 1953 arrangements. In an attempt to ease the rolling stock position on Friday nights, the ER and NER raised the possibility of splitting the Marylebone departures; 'parent' trains again departing on Fridays, but 'extras' leaving mid-week. This proposal would alleviate, to some extent, the shortage of coaches on Friday nights, and increase the utilisation of Starlight stock. For the same reasons both these regions also suggested that, as loadings had been relatively light for a few weeks after Easter in 1954, the introduction of the weekly facility (from Marylebone) in 1955 should be deferred until Friday 3 June.

However, after due consideration from both the commercial and operating departments, both these ER/NER proposals were rejected. The main objective of the Starlight service was to compete with overnight road services, and as the preponderance of this holiday traffic arose at weekends, any break in the provision of a rail alternative, or transfer of rail capacity away from weekends would materially lessen the effectiveness of rail's counteraction to the road competition.

In an attempt to improve the utilisation of Starlight rolling stock in general, consideration was also given to a suggestion that both English and Scottish originating traffic should operate outward on Saturday nights, with a return on Sunday nights. From an operating department aspect this would certainly have advantages, but from the commercial department standpoint the attractiveness of the Starlight facility would be compromised for the following reasons:

1. Many of the passengers vulnerable to road competition desire to begin their journeys on Friday nights, a practice that had become more widespread with the introduction of the five-day week.
2. Onward connections beyond London, or Glasgow/Edinburgh, would not be as good on a Sunday morning.
3. Return journeys arriving back on Monday mornings would be wholly unacceptable to those returning to work, these people forming the vast majority of travellers.
4. Boarding house accommodation was usually booked Saturday–Saturday particularly during peak holiday periods.

The above reasons were felt to apply with greater force in Scotland than in England, and the chief commercial manager (ScR) deprecated any attempt to introduce this 'Saturday out/ Sunday back' option. As a compromise, it was also proposed that Friday night operations be restricted to one east coast departure (using King's Cross) and two on the west coast route, in both directions, with overflow traffic running on Saturday. Based on 1954 loadings this arrangement would deny no less than 26,000 Scottish holidaymakers the opportunity to travel on Fridays during the July and August period. This idea was therefore rejected by the ScR, though the possibility that on weekends of heavy demand extra outward Starlights might run on Saturday nights to cater for passengers who could not be accommodated on Fridays was worth consideration (but return travel would remain on Saturday).

Discussion of these various proposals had been protracted and it was not until 24 February that the BTC made the final decisions on the key issues. These were that:

- the services to remain on Friday/Saturday nights as hitherto
- trains on the St Pancras/Glasgow service will again all be formed of compartment stock
- on the east coast route compartment stock will be provided for at least the first and second excursions on any night
- a survey of the coaching stock position has been put in hand, urgently, so that the best means can be found of meeting the additional commitment imposed on the east coast route
- fares will remain at 1954 levels
- advance bookings to open 14 March 1955 (except for Edinburgh Trades Holiday (1 July) and Glasgow Fair Holiday (15 July), for which bookings commence 21 March. Publicity material to be made available as tabulated below:

	ER	LMR	NER	ScR	SR	WR
Handbills	20,000	50,000	*	50,000	15,000	25,000
D/R posters	250	600	*	1,500	700	200
D/C posters	125	300	*	1,000	500	100
16 sheet posters	**175	50	*	100	125	50
4 sheet (van side) posters	150	350	*	200	150	100
Show cards	40	50	*	75	30	50

* Small quantity required will be obtained from ScR
** 100 to be forwarded to London Transport Executive
D/R = Double Royal size
D/C = Double Crown size

In addition, the British Transport Commission reiterated its view that in planning the Starlight facility the first consideration should be the provision of a high standard service at an attractive charge to minimise the effect of road competition over the Anglo-Scottish route. In this regard, the Road Services Report for 1954 concluded that although some transfer of business from Scottish Omnibuses to rail did occur, the effect was not substantial. Contrastingly, from observations of Northern Roadways loadings during 1954, these were significantly less than in either of the two previous years. The commission therefore concluded that the overnight rail service had both successfully deterred the independent road operator, and fostered extra long distance rail travel. The commission also viewed with satisfaction that rail bookings between London and Glasgow/Edinburgh at fares other than Starlight levels showed increases of 4 to 5 per cent during the 1954 summer season.

"STARLIGHT SPECIAL"

An additional 'Train has been arranged for the "Holiday Fortnight"

FRI. 9th JULY... Dep. ABERDEEN   4.25 p.m.
FRI. 9th JULY... Dep. STONEHAVEN   4.50 p.m.
SAT. 10th JULY Arr. MARYLEBONE   6.30 a.m.

SAT. 24th JULY Dep. MARYLEBONE 10.15 p.m.
SUN. 25th JULY Arr. STONEHAVEN 11.55 a.m. (approx.)
SUN. 25th JULY Arr. ABERDEEN   12.20 p.m. (approx.)

CAFETERIA CAR — RESERVED SEATS
FARE — £5 - 8 - 4 RETURN
(Stonehaven £5-3-8)

Munro's Tourist Agency

12 CROWN STREET   130 UNION STREET
ABERDEEN — 20358   ABERDEEN — 29373

An advertisement published in a local paper on 18 May 1954 for 'Starlight' starting at Aberdeen. Add-on fare was £5 8s 4d less £3 10s = £1 18s 4d to/from Edinburgh. (Courtesy Scottish Railway Preservation Society)

BRITISH TRANSPORT COMMISSION

No. D **70**

No. D **7051**

Issued at .... *4853.* ....

Date of Outward Journey *23/7/54*

E to

CUT FOR CHILD

"STARLIGHT SPECIAL"

RETURN JOURNEY   3rd CLASS

LONDON
(MARYLEBONE)
TO
EDINBURGH
(WAVERLEY)

Available only by *10.75* p.m. train from London (Marylebone)
on Saturday .... *July 3/st...* 195*4*.

FARE 70s. 0d.

COACH .... *D/0.*

SEAT No. .... *5*   FACING ENGINE/BACK TO ENGINE

NOT TRANSFERABLE. Issued subject to the Regulations and Conditions in the Commission's Publications and Notices applicable to the British Railways. Not available for break of journey.
BR 3505/4

A dated ticket for the return leg from Marylebone for an eight-day holiday originating in Scotland. It would be interesting to know which station '4853' referred to. (Brian Pask)

610

SATURDAY, 5th June—*Continued.*

STRENGTHENING OF PASSENGER TRAINS—Continued.

Departure Time	To	Details of Strengthening	Total Tonnage of Train	Remarks
Keith Town				
12-20 p.m.	Aberdeen	2 TK	—	
London St Pancras				
9-0 a.m.	Edinburgh Waverley ...	1 TK	—	
Mallaig				
7-42 a.m.	Glasgow Queen Street ...	1 TK	176	
		2 TK	317	Attached Fort William.
1-0 p.m.	Glasgow Queen Street ...	1 TK	198	
		1 TK	347	Attached Fort William.
Perth				
3-27 p.m.	Edinburgh Waverley ...	1 TK	322	
7-50 p.m.	Edinburgh Waverley ...	1 TK	293	
York				
6-40 a.m.	Edinburgh Wzverley ...	3 TK	—	
10-5 a.m.	Edinburgh Waverley ...	1 TK	—	

BERWICK TO EDINBURGH WAVERLEY AND GLASGOW QUEEN STREET H.L.

	A	A	A	A	C	A	A	A	A
	401	370	92	96	2	372	392	378	369
								4S1	5S12
		(4th) p.m.	(4th) p.m.	(4th) p.m.		(4th)	(4th) p.m.		
London K. Cr. ... dep	...	7 5	7 15	7 30	...	10 20	...	...	...
London M'bone dep	...	...	...	...	...	...	9 45	...	...
Leeds City	9 55	...	...	...	...	...	...	...	...
	a.m.	a.m.	a.m.	a.m.	a.m.	a.m.	a.m.	a.m.	a.m.
Berwick	1 37	2 1	2 15	2 32	3 51	5 12	5 55	8 28	11 30
Marshall Meadows	1 39	2 3	2 17	2 34	3 54	5 14	5 57	8 30	11 32
Reston Jn.	1 51	2 15	2 29	2 46	4 9	5 26	6 8	8 43	11 43
Grantshouse	1 58	2 22	2 37	2 54	4 18	5 34	6 14	8 52	11 50
Dunbar	2 9	2 34	2 49	3 6	4 33	5 46	6 25	9 4	12 4p
Drem Jn.	2 21	2 46	3 1	3 18	4 47	5 59	6 35	9 16	12 17
Longniddry	...	...	...	...	4 52	...	...	...	...
Monktonhall Jn.	2 35	2 58	3 13	3 33	5 0	6 15	6 45	9 30	12 31
Portobello	2 41	3 4	3 19	3 39	5 6	6 21	6 51	9 36	12 37
Piershill	...	...	...	...	...	...	...	9 40	...
Edinburgh Wav. arr	2 47	3 10	3 25	3 45	5 13	6 28	6 57	...	12 43
Do. dep	2 57	3 20	3 40	4 5	...	6†43	7†10	11 vehs.	12†55
Haymarket	3 0	...	...	...	...	6 48	7 15	incl.	13 vehs.
Gorgie East	...	...	...	...	12-25a	6 51	7 18	RB	430 tons
Niddrie West Jn.	10 vehs.	Relief	12 vehs.	7-0p	Parcels	7 10	7 38	390 tons	...
Niddrie North Jn.	330 tons	to	incl.	Ordy.	York	7 13	7 40	...	...
Portobello	...	Aber-	410 tons	London	to	7 15	7 42	...	...
Craigentinny CS arr	...	deen	...	K. Cr.	Edin.	7†18	7†45	...	...
Bathgate Jn.	3 9	12 vehs.	...	to	Wav.	Relief	Star-	...	...
Winchburgh Jn.	3 15	410 tons	...	Aber-	retimed	12 vehs.	light	...	...
Polmont	3 27	...	...	deen	...	400 tons	11 vehs.	...	...
Greenhill Upper Jn.	3 36	...	...	retimed	...	...	incl.	...	...
Lenzie Jn.	3 49	...	...	...	...	...	Cafe	...	...
Cowlairs West Jn.	3 56	...	...	...	...	...	Car	...	...
Glas. Q.S. H.L. arr	4 3	...	...	...	...	...	360 tons	...	...
	† to Cowlairs	Forward times on page 617	Forward times on page 617	Forward times on page 617		† to Saughton arr.	† form 448	† dep. 9-40a to C'tinny	† to Niddrie West

An extract from Special Traffic Notice for Saturday 5 June 1954. Page 610 shows Down train 392 ex-Marylebone; stock to form Up train 448 (page 612, overleaf) scheduled from Waverley at 9.40 p.m., but with a footnote showing this to be retimed. (BRB Residuary)

612

SATURDAY, 5th June—Continued.

GLASGOW QUEEN STREET AND EDINBURGH WAVERLEY TO BERWICK.

	A	A	A	A	A	A	C	A			
	434	51	102	424	425	416	265	448			
	Spare Set † of 364 C'tinny dep. 9-40a			Spare Set † dep. Cowlairs 11-40a	† of 400	† of 416a dep. C'tinny 8†17p	Previous times on page 61	† of 392 dep. C'tinny 8†58p			
	a.m.	a.m.	a.m.	p.m.	p.m.	p.m.	p.m.	p.m.			
Rutherglen .... dep	...	...	10 16	...	...	...	...	...	...	...	...
Glas. Q.S. H.L. dep	...	...		12 20	3 40	...	...	...	...	...	...
Cowlairs West Jn. ...	...	...	Garex	12 27	3 47	...	...	...	...	...	...
Lenzie Jn.	...	...	9 vehs.	12 32½	3 52½	...	...	...	...	...	...
Greenhill Upper Jn. ...	...	...	270 tons	12 45	4 5	...	4-45p	Star-	...	...	...
Falkirk High	Relief	8-35a	...	12 52	...	Relief	Q Fish	light	...	...	...
Carmuirs West Jn. ...	12 vehs.	Ordy.	11 0	...	...		A'deen	11 vehs.	...	...	...
Carmuirs East Jn. ...	incl.	Gl'gow	11 1	...	...	...	to	incl.	...	...	...
Falkirk G'ston arr	TTO	Qn. St.	11L 5	...	...	...	London	Cafeteria	...	...	...
Do. dep	RB	H.L.	11 8	...	...	...	K. Cr.	Car	...	...	...
Polmont	TTO	to	11 15	12 59	4 12½	...	(Susp.)	360 tons	...	...	...
Linlithgow	(fluid)	London	...	1 7	...	...	running	...	...	...	...
Winchburgh Jn.	396 tons	K. Cr.	11 26	1 14	4 23	...	if	...	...	...	...
Bathgate Jn.	...	retimed	11 32	1 21½	4 29	...	required	...	...	...	...
Haymarket West Jn. ...	...	...	11 40	...	...	...	and	...	...	...	...
Gorgie East Jn.	...	...	11 43	...	...	...	retimed	...	...	...	...
Niddrie West Jn. ...	...	...	11 58	...	...	...	...	...	...	...	...
Haymarket	...	...	...	1 31	4 37	...	8 55	...	...	...	...
Edinburgh Wav. arr	9†48	...	...	1 35	4 40	8†25	9 0	9† 8	...	...	...
Do. dep	10 10	10 20	...	1 45	4 55	9 0	9 10	9 40	...	...	...
Portobello............	10 16	10 26	12 4p	1 51	5 1	9 6	9 16	9 46	...	...	...
Monktonhall Jn.	10 21	10 31	...	1 56	5 6	9 12	9 22	9 51	...	...	...
Drem Jn.	10 33	10 43	...	2 8	5 18	9 24	9 36	10 2	...	...	...
Dunbar	10 44	10 56	...	2 19	5 32	9 35	9 51	10 12	...	...	...
Grantshouse	11 2	11 17	...	2 35	5 51	9 49	10 10	10 26	...	...	...
Reston Jn.	11 8	11 23	...	2 40	5 56	9 55	10 16	10 31	...	...	...
Marshall Meadows	11 18	11 33	...	2 50	6 6	10 6	10 28	10 40	...	...	...
Berwick .... arr	11 20	11 36	...	2 53	6 9	10 8	10 31	10 42	...	...	...
Tynemouth ...... arr	...	...	...	...	...	...	...	...	...	...	...
Newcastle .... arr	12 43p	12 56p	...	4 9	7 28	11 33	...	...	...	...	...
Durham .... arr	...	1 24	...	...	...	...	...	...	...	...	...
Darlington .... arr	1 40	1 56	...	5 2	...	...	...	...	...	...	...
York .... arr	2 32	2 45	...	5 57	...	...	...	...	...	...	...
Peterborough ... arr	4 42	4 52	...	...	...	...	...	...	...	...	...
London K. Cr. ... arr	6 20	6 36	...	...	...	...	...	...	...	...	...
London M'bone arr	...	...	...	...	...	...	...	6 50a	...	...	...
			† dep. 12†7p arr. C'tinny C.S. 12†10p form 310				Tweedmouth arr. 10-36p dep. 10-50p				

102—Will be worked by through engine. Trainmen with Conductors between Falkirk Grahamston and Portobello.

424—12-20 p.m. Ordinary, Glasgow Queen Street H.L. to Edinburgh Waverley, retimed and extended to York. 11 vehicles, including RT and BTO attach at Edinburgh—354 tons.
Engine to work through Glasgow Queen Street to Newcastle.
11-52 a.m. Ordinary, Hyndland to Edinburgh Waverley, to depart Haymarket 1-36 p.m., arrive Edinburgh Waverley 1-40 p.m.

425—Relief. 10 vehicles, including TTO, RB, TTO (fluid)—340 tons. 4-7 p.m. (Parcels) Falkirk Grahamston to Polmont to arrive 4-16 p.m.

448—9-28 p.m. E.C.S., Craigentinny to Edinburgh Waverley, to depart 9-33 p.m. and arrive Edinburgh Waverley 9-43 p.m.
9-35 p.m. E.C.S. Edinburgh Waverley to Craigentinny, to run via Lochend Jn.

LONDON
to
GLASGOW & EDINBURGH

"STARLIGHT SPECIAL"

70/-
RETURN
(including Reserved Seats)

Thursday, 7th April and Friday nights
from 15th April to 23rd September inclusive

★

STAY 8 OR 15 DAYS

★

EXPRESS NIGHT TRAVEL

★

BUFFET AVAILABLE

★

CHILDREN HALF FARE

★

ADVANCE BOOKINGS ESSENTIAL

FULL DETAILS ON OTHER SIDE

★ **STARLIGHT SPECIAL TRAINS,** one class only, will run on Thursday, 7th April, Friday, 15th April, thereafter every Friday to 23rd September inclusive, from London to Glasgow and London to Edinburgh. Passengers will return by Special trains on Saturday nights the 8th or 15th day after arrival (the 9th or 16th day in the case of passengers departing on 7th April).

★ **STARLIGHT SPECIAL TRAINS** assure seats to all passengers. Accommodation is limited and for this reason it is **essential** that passengers *BOOK IN ADVANCE STATING THE DATE ON WHICH THEY DESIRE TO TRAVEL FORWARD AND RETURN.*

★ **STARLIGHT SPECIAL TRAINS** are available **only** to holders of Starlight Special tickets specifying the appropriate train and date of travel.

★ **STARLIGHT SPECIAL TRAINS** run as shown below, and light refreshments are obtainable.

OUTWARD JOURNEY FRIDAY NIGHTS	RETURN JOURNEY SATURDAY NIGHTS
London St. Pancras dep. 11.00 p.m.	Glasgow St. Enoch dep. 8.35 p.m.
Glasgow St. Enoch arr. 9.35 a.m.	London St. Pancras arr. 7.12 a.m.
London Marylebone dep. 9.45 p.m.	Edinburgh Waverley dep. 9.40 p.m.
Edinburgh Waverley arr. 6.57 a.m.	London Marylebone arr. 6.53 a.m.*
	*7.18 a.m. from 19th June to 18th September inclusive

★ **STARLIGHT SPECIAL TRAIN TICKETS,** are on sale at London Terminal Stations, also at principal suburban stations, Railway Ticket Offices and Ticket Agencies in the London area. Remittances for the fare, 70/- which includes a reserved seat in each direction (half fare for children aged 3 but under 14 years), must accompany all postal applications to :

FOR BOOKINGS TO GLASGOW :

Enquiry Office, St. Pancras Station, London, N.W.1

FOR BOOKINGS TO EDINBURGH :

Enquiry Office, Marylebone Station, London, N.W.1

★ **STARLIGHT SPECIAL TICKETS ARE NOT TRANSFERABLE** and are issued subject to the bye-laws, regulations and conditions contained in the publications and notices of or applicable to the British Transport Commission. They are not available for break of journey. British Railways do not undertake to refund the value of lost, mislaid or unused tickets. Further information may be obtained on application to :

DISTRICT PASSENGER MANAGER, *Euston Station, London, N.W.1*

DISTRICT OPERATING SUPERINTENDENT, *Paddington Station, London, W.2*

TRAVEL LIGHT — SEND YOUR LUGGAGE IN ADVANCE

For Passengers who prefer a Combined Road Rail facility to Glasgow or Edinburgh by ordinary services (out by road, return by rail or vice versa) tickets are obtainable at a fare of 80/- from Scottish Omnibuses Ltd., 298 Regent Street, London, W.1, who will supply details on request.

PUBLISHED BY THE BRITISH TRANSPORT COMMISSION

55/26

B.R. 35001

BRITISH RAILWAYS

(BRB Residuary)

The 1955 Season

General arrangements:

From London the season began on Thursday 7 April, and then Fridays 15 April to 23 September inclusive.

From Glasgow/Edinburgh the season began on Fridays 8 April to 23 September inclusive.

Typical intermediate timing as follows:

Thursday 7 April		*Friday 8 April*	
Marylebone dep 9.45 p.m.		Waverley dep. 9.40 p.m.	
Leicester (C)	11.58 p.m./12.4 a.m. (L)	Newcastle	11.56 p.m./12.4 a.m. (L)
Rotherwood Sidings	1.25 a.m./1.31 a.m. (W)*	York	1.28 a.m./1.35 a.m. (L)
		Rotherwood Sidings	3.0 a.m./3.6 a.m. (W*)
York	2.56 a.m./3.4 a.m. (L)		
Newcastle	4.35 a.m./4.44 a.m. (L)	Leicester (C)	4.26 a.m./4.33 a.m. (L)
Waverley arr.	6.57 a.m.	Mar'bone arr. 6.49 a.m.	

Formation; BTK/4TK/CC/4TK/BTK   Formation; 7 bogies only inc. CC

L = loco change
W = loco water stop
* = on other dates, W at Rotherham (C) or Pontefract (Baghill) or Mexborough

Number of Starlights run during the season from each terminal

a. St Pancras–St Enoch; not more than four on any one night.
b. St Enoch–St Pancras; as above except:
   1 July, eight to St Pancras plus three to Euston
   15 July, seven to St Pancras plus two to Euston
   29 July, seven to St Pancras plus four to Euston (three start at Paisley)

All the above were formed of compartment stock, except three trains from Glasgow on 15 July when LMR supplied open stock. Also on this date the whole of the traffic booked could not be accommodated and the overflow was conveyed (for the first time) in two specials run on Saturday 16 July.

c. Marylebone–Waverley; winter timetable, 'parent' plus one 'Q' (conditional) train summer timetable, maximum of four on any one night.

d. Waverley–Marylebone, as above except:

1 July, six trains 8 July, six trains
15 July, six trains 22 July; five trains

Compartment stock was provided for the 'parent' and first duplicate. Additional trains were of open stock.

On either route, outward or return, cafeteria car provision was again restricted to a maximum of two per night, with brake van service for all others. Arrangements made in 1954 to start certain trains back at, for instance, Dundee, Kirkcaldy and Aberdeen were repeated.

Early season bookings, Easter weekend to Whit weekend (outward):

Date	Marylebone	St Pancras	Total	St Enoch	Waverley	Total
Thur Apr 7	215	374	589			
8				376	134	510
15	105	130	235	113	41	154
22	43*	79	122	96	29*	125
29	65*	106	171	144	41*	185
May 6	98	82	180	127	55*	182
13	100	145	245	205	54*	259
20	138	123	261	288	100	388
27	292	388	680	275	99	374

returning passengers from:

Date	Marylebone	St Pancras	Total	St Enoch	Waverley	Total
Sat Apr 16	87	287	374	200	116	316
23	68*	156	224	247	178	425
30	41*	117	158	103	56*	159
May 7	45*	103	148	88	49*	137
14	66*	136	202	87	77	164
21	47	147	194	126	115	241
28	93**	288	381	120	112**	232

* Starlight cancelled – passengers conveyed by ordinary service
** Starlight cancelled due to strike by footplate staff (ASLEF)

Between Easter and Whitsuntide, bookings were again low on the east coast route and, as seen from the table, six outward Starlights (and their return workings) were cancelled and passengers conveyed to and from King's Cross by ordinary overnight service. (Thus losing their cafeteria car facility!)

The ASLEF strike began at midnight on Saturday 28 May and was not called off until 6 p.m. on Monday 14 June. The threat of strike action undoubtedly had a severe effect on bookings for April, May and June. Bookings were suspended during the strike period, and all seven Starlights cancelled between Saturday 28 May and Saturday 11 June inclusive, booked passengers again being conveyed by ordinary services.

After the strike was over, the working timetable (current 13 June–18 September) was showing the following 'parent' trains and first duplicate on the west coast route.

Down trains

Fridays		**Fridays (to 2 September)**	
M193		M197	
St Pancras dep. 11.0 p.m.		St Pancras dep. 11.20 p.m.	
Leicester	1.1 a.m. (Saturday)	Leicester	1.27 a.m. (Saturday)
Trent	1.27 a.m.	Trent	1.54 a.m.

plus M585 dep. 11.40 p.m. and M586 dep. 12.00 midnight as necessary

Saturdays		**Saturdays**	
M193		M197	
St Pancras dep. 10.40 p.m.		St Pancras dep. 10.50 p.m.	
Leicester	12.39 a.m. (Sun)	Leicester	12.50 p.m. (Sun)
Trent	1.3 a.m.	Trent	1.13 a.m.

Up trains

Fridays and Saturdays (same times)			
M4		M6	
St Enoch dep. 8.15 p.m.		St Enoch dep. 8.35 p.m.	
Trent	4.17 a.m.	Trent	4.41 a.m.
Leicester	4.43 a.m.	Leicester	5.8 a.m.
St Pancras	6.52 a.m.	St Pancras	7.12 a.m.

plus, for instance:

C605
Galashiels dep. 8.5 p.m. (Friday 29 July)
Trent   3.22 a.m.
St Pancras   6.3 a.m. (Saturday 30 July)

(The full range of Starlights actually run only appeared within the weekly special traffic notices.)

Interestingly, on this same weekend (29/30 July) train formation for the Up Waverley duplicates on Friday was given as BTO/4TO/BTK/4TO/BTO, i.e. open stock throughout except for the central refreshment vehicle. Returning specials to Edinburgh on Saturday 30 July ran as follows:

Train	Marylebone dep.	Waverley arr.
376	10.15 p.m.	7.42 a.m.
377	10.55 p.m.	8.20 a.m.
389	11.30 p.m.	9.12 a.m.
390	11.45 p.m.	9.30 a.m.

On the last day for return of fifteen-day passengers (8 October), reservations were again comparatively few, resulting in the Starlight being cancelled, passengers travelling in ordinary trains.

Financial Results

	1955			1954		
From	Receipts £	Costs £	Profit £	Receipts £	Costs £	Profit £
St Pancras	46,133	19,228	26,905	50,608	20,871	29,737
Marylebone	41,907	16,807	25,100	52,598	17,131	35,437
St Enoch	95,185	30,269	64,916	96,054	32,199	63,855
Waverley	57,769	19,383	38,386	74,972	21,003	53,969
Totals	240,994	85,687	155,307	274,232	91,204	183,028
Deduct 15%			13,000			
Deduct refunds			11,000			10,000
Est net profit			131,307			173,028

* Costs for 1955 were based on figures supplied by the traffic costing service in 1953. The additional sum deducted from profits represents increased costs subsequent to 1953.

These financial results must also be seen in the light of the overall effects of the ASLEF strike as outlined earlier. Further, the late commencement of bookings for 1955 (six weeks later than 1954) had a detrimental effect, and an increase in refunds due to cancellations should also be taken into account.

Friday 17 June. 45568 *Western Australia* at the head of M592, the 7.10 p.m. from St Enoch running via Dalry and Kilmarnock, passing through Shields Road station. The cafeteria car stands out as the sixth vehicle. (W. A. C. Smith/Transport Treasury)

Friday 1 July. 45704 *Leviathan* on M592 again passing the now-closed Bellahouston station, with further roof-boarded 'Starlight Special' stock in the adjacent carriage sidings. (J. L. Stevenson)

More detailed results are again available as in the table below.

From	Trains Out/Rtn	Tickets Adult Child	Receipts £	Loaded Mileage £	Cost per Mile £	Train Cost £	Adv Cost £	Admin Cost £	Profit £
St P	39/42	12,087 2,188	46,133	34,551	10s 2d	17,563	1,100	555	26,905
M'ne	37/37	11,098 1,751	41,907	30,969	9s 9d	15,097	1,100	600	25,100
St E	66/67	25,883 2,625	95,185	56,725	9s 11d	28,126	1,100	1,033	64,916
Wav	43/43	15,467 2,076	57,769	35,991	9s 9d	17,546	1,100	727	38,386
Total	185/189	64,535 8,640	240,994	158,236		78,332	4,400	2,915	155,307
1954 figures	196/189	73,793 9,118	274,232	169,667		84,009	4,100	3,095	183,028

Friday 8 July. 45687 *Neptune* passing Hillington East on M6, the 8.35 p.m. from St Enoch. (W. A. C. Smith/Transport Treasury)

Friday 15 July. Smartly turned out 40573 pilots a grimy unidentified 'Jubilee' through Strathbungo on M593. The pilot will be detached at New Cumnock. (W. A. C. Smith/Transport Treasury)

Friday 29 July. 40566 pilots 45118, again through Strathbungo heading W534, the 7.55 p.m. from St Enoch and one of four 'Starlights' running to Euston that night. (W. A. C. Smith/ Transport Treasury)

From the above data it will be seen that although the west coast route receipts fell by only 3 per cent, the east coast receipts slumped by 22 per cent. This was largely attributed to the negative public reaction to the use of open stock on these services during 1954 and the bad publicity that ensued. Overall, the number of passengers carried was down by roughly 12 per cent.

The Hotels & Catering Services (refreshment rooms department) registered gross takings of £11,675 (£13,457 last year) from service of light refreshments.

As was the case in 1954, no adverse effect on ordinary full-fare bookings on the Anglo-Scottish routes was noted as a result of the Starlight facility, even though ordinary fares were increased by 7.5 per cent from 5 June 1955.

Observations of train workings throughout the 1955 season

1. Friday 8 April 5MT + 45739 *Ulster* head the 8.35 p.m. St Enoch–St Pancras as far as Leeds.
2. Friday 15 April 45687 *Neptune* heads same train, again as far Leeds.
3. Friday 3 June (ASLEF strike period) for passengers with southbound tickets from Scotland, BR gave this advice: Starlight tickets valid on ANY train after midday Friday 3 June and ALL trains tomorrow (Saturday) departing from Glasgow (Central) or Edinburgh (Waverley), suggested trains being: Friday ex-Central 2.00 p.m., 9.45 p.m., 11.55 p.m.; Friday ex-Waverley 1.30 p.m., 6.15 p.m., 11.0 p.m., but there will be no reserved seating available.
4. Friday 17 June, 45568 *Western Australia* works M592, the 7.10 p.m. from St Enoch, via Dalry and Kilmarnock, to Leeds.
5. Saturday 18 June, 61009 *Hartebeeste* brings Starlight into York from Leicester; takes York–Sheffield ECS working on Monday 20th.
6. Friday 1 July departures from St Enoch:
   45704 *Leviathan* heads M592 (above)
   73059 + 72000 *Clan Buchanan* head the Gourock–St Pancras
   46222 *Queen Mary* heads the 7.55 p.m., via Barrhead
   42202 – due to engine failure – heads the 9.23 p.m. via Canal Line and is replaced at Corkerhill.
7. Friday 8 July, 45687 *Neptune* heads M6, the 8.35 p.m. from St Enoch.
8. Friday 15 July, 40573 + 'Jubilee' head south at Strathbungo.
9. Saturday 16 July, 60863 arrives at York from Leicester and, as usual, heads the 8.35 a.m. York–Newcastle fill-in turn.
10. Friday 29 July, 40566 + 45118 pass Strathbungo on W534, the 7.50 p.m. from St Enoch.
11. Saturday 30 July, 60070 *Gladiateur* seen at Cockburnspath working between Newcastle and Waverley.
12. Friday 5 August, 44706 passes Bellahouston on the 7.10 p.m. from St Enoch.
13. Friday 23 September, 45707 *Valiant* heads the last Up train from St Enoch.

LONDON
BY
STARLIGHT SPECIAL

EVERY FRIDAY NIGHT
From 8th April to 23rd September, 1955

70/- Return Fare
Third Class **70/-**
Children half fare

Lve. Glasgow 8.35 p.m. ‖ Lve. Edinburgh 9.40 p.m.
(St. Enoch) ‖ (Waverley)

STAY 8 OR 15 DAYS
EXPRESS NIGHT TRAVEL
FARE INCLUDES RESERVED SEAT
NIGHT BUFFET AVAILABLE
ADVANCE BOOKING ESSENTIAL

Booking opens on Monday, 14th March, for all Fridays except
Edinburgh Trades Holiday Friday (1st July) and Glasgow
Fair Friday (15th July).

Booking opens on Monday, 21st March, for Edinburgh Trades
Holiday Friday (1st July) and Glasgow Fair Friday
(15th July).

Full details from Railway Stations, Offices and Agencies.

BRITISH RAILWAYS

(BRB Residuary)

The 1956 Season

Having resolved, at some length, the coaching stock problem on the Marylebone–Waverley trains at the end of the previous year, discussions on the forthcoming arrangements for 1956 were more brisk. It was soon agreed that a fare increase to 75s was appropriate and that the operating season was to be Thursday 29 March (Maundy Thursday) from London and thereafter on Fridays 30 March to 21 September inclusive from Scotland.

Rolling stock arrangements were to be as agreed for 1955 and, to coincide with annual holidays, some ScR-originating Starlights would again start back from selected points. 'Train Attendants' were to be paid at the ticket collector rate of 155s per week throughout the operating season.

However, it was pointed out once more that loadings in the immediate post-Easter period were again light. The running of a combined Glasgow and Edinburgh to Marylebone train (in conjunction with a direct St Enoch–St Pancras service on 30 March only) was therefore considered favourably for five weeks from 6 April to 4 May, after which the normal schedule of trains would be adopted. The snag was that a heavy programme of engineering work was to take place on the GC main line between Woodford Halse and Leicester, necessitating closure to traffic on Sundays throughout the period of the proposed combined trains to Marylebone. This would involve return traffic from Scotland on Saturday being dealt with at King's Cross rather than Marylebone. After a second look at these proposals from both the commercial and operating departments, it was decided that it would be simpler if the combined trains were to run, as far as possible, into St Pancras rather than either of the other two termini. Early season provision was therefore to be as follows (subject to traffic demands):

	From London	From Scotland
Thur 29 March	Marylebone–Waverley	
	St Pancras–St Enoch	
Friday 30 March		St E and Wav – M'bone
		St Enoch–St Pancras

Friday 30 March. 60534 *Irish Elegance* gets the 1956 season underway on Good Friday, heading the combined train to Marylebone at St Enoch's platform 2, ready to depart at 8.15 p.m. (J. L. Stevenson)

Friday 6 April	Marylebone–Waverley St Pancras–St Enoch	St E and Wav – Marylebone
Saturday 7 April	St P–Wav and Queen St (HL)	Waverley–King's Cross
Friday 13 April	Marylebone–Waverley St Pancras–St Enoch	St E and Wav – St Pancras
Saturday 14 Apr	St P – Wav and Queen St (LL)	Waverley–King's Cross St Enoch–St Pancras
Friday 20 April	St P – Wav and St Enoch	St E and Wav – St Pancras
Saturday 21 Apr	St P – Wav and Queen St (LL)	St E and Wav – St Pancras
Friday 27 April	St P – Wav and St Enoch	St E and Wav – St Pancras
Saturday 28 Apr	St P – Wav and Queen St (LL)	St E and Wav – St Pancras
Friday 4 May	St P – Wav and St Enoch	St E and Wav – St Pancras
Saturday 5 May	St P – Wav and Queen St (LL)	St E and Wav – St Pancras
Friday 11 May	Marylebone–Waverley St Pancras–St Enoch	St E and Wav – St Pancras St Enoch–St Pancras
Saturday 12 May	Marylebone–Waverley St Pancras–Queen St (LL)	Waverley–King's Cross St Enoch–St Pancras

Notes

- St Enoch closed on Sundays.
- Combined trains after 6 April routed via Waverley/Newcastle/York/Wath Road Junction and Rotherham, thence to St Pancras.
- Engineering work diverts three up Saturday night Starlights to King's Cross.
- Combined trains also run later in the season as bookings dictated.

Early season workings and observations

Friday 30 March

The first Down train arrives at St Enoch thirty-eight minutes late at 10.20 a.m. behind 45605 *Cyprus* having hauled the St Pancras train from Leeds. The first Up working to St Pancras departs St Enoch at 8.35 p.m. behind 46102 *Black Watch* (66A) running via Barrhead. The combined train leaves St Enoch at 8.15 p.m. for Edinburgh with 60534 *Irish Elegance* as power (Haymarket (64B) engine with Eastfield crew to Waverley, loco working to Newcastle), heading for Marylebone.

The running of combined trains therefore brought LNER Pacifics into St Enoch on a scheduled basis for the first time. These trains also traversed the Saltmarket curve to exit St Enoch (not used regularly for passenger traffic since pre-Grouping days) and headed for Cowlairs, Polmont and Edinburgh. Departing Waverley at 9.40 p.m., Marylebone was due to be reached at 6.53 a.m. Saturday morning.

The first service from Marylebone (dep. 9.45 p.m. Thursday 29th) reaches Waverley at 7.27 a.m.

Friday 6 April

Combined train (TRN 446) leaves St Enoch behind 60043 *Brown Jack*.

Saturday 7 April

The first train (447) diverted to King's Cross leaves Waverley at 9.40 p.m., reaching London at 6.30 a.m. Sunday morning. The first trains (M193) diverted away from St Enoch were on the 7th and 14th.

St Pancras dep. 10.40 p.m. (7th)		10.40 p.m. (14th)
Newcastle dep. 5.44 a.m.		5.30 a.m. (Sunday)
Waverley dep. 8.4/8.20 a.m.		7.17/7.29 a.m.
Queen St (HL) 9.33 a.m.	Queen St (LL)	8.44 a.m.

Formation of M193: BTK/4TK/CC/4TK/BTK of eleven coaches (at 345tons) of LMS stock.

Saturday 21 April, 44944 heads 11 p.m. (Fri) ex-St Pancras; Sheffield–Newcastle.
Saturday 28 April, 45664 *Nelson* heads 11 p.m. (Fri) ex-St Pancras; Sheffield–Newcastle.
Saturday 5 May, 45656 *Cochrane* heads 11 p.m. (Fri) ex-St Pancras; Sheffield–Newcastle.
Saturday 12 May, 45656 *Cochrane* heads 11 p.m. (Fri) ex-St Pancras; Sheffield–Newcastle. (All trains M193.)

These Millhouses (Sheffield) engines were serviced at 52A (Gateshead) before returning to Sheffield on the southbound Starlight (dep. St Enoch 8.35 p.m. Saturday night), i.e. engines being changed at Sheffield and Newcastle in both directions.

Saturday 28 April, 60509 *Waverley* brings combined train into St Enoch.
Friday 11 May, 60100 *Spearmint* takes 8 p.m. combined train out of St Enoch.
Friday 25 May, 60519 *Honeyway* takes combined train (M4) from St Enoch heading for Edinburgh, Newcastle and Marylebone.

Later workings and observations

Friday 29 June
73056 + 45692 *Cyclops* head St Pancras-bound Starlight originating at Gourock. Pilot to New Cumnock only.

Friday 11 May. Six weeks later and it's 60100 *Spearmint* that heads the 8.15 p.m. in rather more favourable lighting conditions. (W. A. C. Smith/Transport Treasury)

BR had, on 3 June, redesignated '3rd class' as '2nd class'; consequently descriptions of coaching stock became BSK for Brake Second Corridor rather than BTK for Brake Third Corridor.

Friday 6 July

On this date the maximum number of specials (6) left Waverley.

M591	Waverley dep.	6.30 p.m.		445	Waverley dep.	7.32 p.m.
	Hawick	7.48/7.54 p.m			Newcastle	10.8 p.m.
	Carlisle	9.6/9.14 p.m.			Marylebone	5.39 a.m. (Sat)
	St Pancras	5.32 a.m. (Saturday)				

Formation: BSK/4SK/BSK/5SK/BSK of eleven coaches (370 tons inc. RB), twelve coaches (372 tons). Central BSK for refreshments.

446	Cardenden dep. 6.10 p.m.	447	Kirkcaldy dep. 7.42 p.m.
	Waverley 7.37/7.50 p.m.		Waverley 8.30/8.53 p.m.
	Marylebone 5.47 a.m. (Saturday)		Marylebone 6.35 a.m. (Saturday)
eleven coaches of 370 tons inc. RB		eleven coaches of 370 tons inc. RB	

448	Waverley dep. 9.5 p.m.	213	Waverley dep. 9.23 p.m.
	Newcastle 11.39 p.m.		Newcastle 11.51 p.m.
	Marylebone 6.58 a.m.		Marylebone 7.29 a.m.

Eleven coaches of 363 tons including the cafeteria car. (RB = Restaurant Buffet, the first time these BR Mk1 vehicles were mentioned as being in use on these trains, if the descriptions in the working timetable are accurate.)

Friday 13 July

Five trains depart from Waverley, 445/6/7/8 as above, plus 213 departing Kirkcaldy at 8.14 p.m. for Waverley at 9.4/9.23 p.m. and M'bone 7.29 a.m. 70051 *Firth of Forth* heads W535, the 9.48 p.m. from St Enoch bound for Euston with Glasgow Fair traffic. First 'Britannia' so used.

Friday 20 July

Waverley departures were as follows:

	447	448	213
Dundee (TB)		dep. 6.13 p.m.	Dundee dep. 7.10 p.m.
Waverley	8.30/8.53 p.m.	dep. 9.5 p.m.	Waverley 9.9/9.23 p.m.
N'castle	11.18 p.m.	11.39 p.m.	Newcastle 11.51 p.m.
Mar'bone	6.35 a.m. (Saturday)	6.58 a.m.	Marylebone 7.29 a.m.

All these departures eleven coaches, 370 tons inc. RB, CC, BSK respectively.

Friday 20/Saturday 21 July
60501 *Cock O' The North* heads one of 447/8, 213 (above) from Newcastle to York.

Saturday 21 July
8.15 p.m. from St Enoch leaves at 9.45 p.m.
8.35 p.m. leaves at 9.55 p.m.
Both due to the all-wheel derailment of 40599 outside St Enoch at 5.30 p.m.

Waverley arrivals, Sunday 22 July

216 M'bone dep. 10.0 p.m.	N'castle 5.30 a.m.	Wav'ley 7.30 a.m.
376 M'bone dep. 10.42 p.m.	N'castle 5.24 a.m.	Wav'ley 7.44 a.m.
377 M'bone dep. 10.55 p.m.	N'castle 6.20 a.m.	Wav'ley 8.20/8.35 a.m.
		K'caldy 9.20 a.m.
378 M'bone dep. 11.30 p.m.	N'castle 7.2 a.m.	Wav'ley 9.21 a.m.
379 M'bone dep. 11.45 p.m.	N'castle 7.16 a.m.	Wav'ley 9.36/9.47 a.m.
		Car'den 11.0 a.m.
M584 St Pancras dep. 11.25 p.m.	Carlisle 7.23 a.m.	Hawick 8.40 a.m.
		Waverley 10.10 a.m.

Trains 216, 376–9 also departed Marylebone at the same times on Saturday 28 July (379 running to Edinburgh only).

Meanwhile, on the west coast route, overflow traffic to/from Euston ran as follows:

Friday 13 July
All fourteen coaches of 435 tons with BSKs for refreshments.

W533	from St Enoch	Crewe 12.53/1.0 a.m. (K)	Euston 4.21 a.m. (Saturday)
W535	from St Enoch	Crewe 4.7/4.19 a.m. (K)	7.30 a.m.
W536	from Coatbridge	Crewe 4.28/4.30 a.m. (K)	7.55 a.m.

(K) indicates stop to replenish BSKs.

Saturday 14 July
W681 Euston 10.22 p.m. to Crewe 1.32/1.40 a.m.
W687 Euston 12.20 a.m. to Crewe 3.51 a.m. (pass)

Both fourteen coaches of 435 tons, both with cafeteria cars.

* * *

Additional southbound Starlights to St Pancras were as follows.

Saturday 14 July
St Enoch dep. 8.15 p.m. (parent) and 8.35 (Q). Formation: BSK/4SK/CAF/5SK/BSK (twelve coaches of 370 tons) plus three further duplicates at 7.45 p.m., 9.23 p.m. and

July. Down trains were rarely photographed, but here is 60088 *Book Law* heading north on Cockburnspath bank with train 448 from Marylebone – a neat rake of Gresley stock.

July. Same place, at much the same time and probably on the same day (about 6.15 a.m.), sees 60030 *Golden Fleece* working train 445 – a similar formation. (Both photos C. J. B. Sanderson/ Armstrong Railway Photographic Trust)

10.20 p.m. with the same formation except that a BSK (for refreshments) replaced the central CAF vehicle.

Friday 27 July
W534 formation BSO/6SO/BSK/5SO/BSO
W534 St Enoch to C'lisle 10.27/10.35 p.m., to Crewe 1.29/1.39 a.m., to Euston 5.18 a.m.
W535 Kil'nock to C'lisle 10.45/10.55 p.m., to Crewe 1.59/2.7 a.m., to Euston 5.38 a.m.
W535 formation BSK/6SO/BSK/5SO/BSK

Saturday 28 July
W693 Euston–Glasgow (Central); Crewe 12.18 a.m. (pass) Carlisle 3.46/3.55 a.m.
W691 Euston dep. 11.50 p.m. to Carstairs, Hamilton, Motherwell, Coatbridge.
W695 Euston 11.55 p.m. – Glasgow (Central), Crewe 3.3/3.11 a.m. Carlisle 6.34/6.45 a.m.

All fourteen coaches of 435 tons, all stated as having cafeteria cars!

The same weekend saw eight Starlights in/out of St Pancras, as follows (all twelve coaches of 372 tons).

Friday 27 July
M585 St Pancras–St Enoch   Carlisle 8.10/8.18 a.m. (Saturday)
M586 St Pancras–St Enoch   Carlisle 8.49/8.55 a.m.
M595 St Enoch–St Pancras   Carlisle 2.14/2.22 a.m.

Saturday 28 July
M583 St Pancras–St Enoch   Carlisle 6.57/7.5 a.m. (Sun)
M584 St Pancras–St Enoch   Carlisle 7.15/7.23 a.m.
M585 St Pancras–St Enoch   Carlisle 7.32/7.40 a.m.
M586 St Pancras–St Enoch   Carlisle 7.50/7.58 a.m.
M594 St Enoch–St Pancras   Carlisle 12.16/12.20 a.m.

Sunday 29 July
45697 *Mars* brings a returning Starlight into St Enoch.
60019 *Bittern* heads a down train between Newcastle and Edinburgh.

Undated July
60088 *Book Law* heads down train 448 on Cockburnspath.
60030 *Golden Fleece* does the same on train 445.

Saturday 11 August
60038 *Firdaussi* works between York and Newcastle on either the 10.40 p.m. (216) or the 11.45 p.m. (381) from Marylebone, Friday 10th.

Passengers boarding one of Marylebone's departures. Note the different style of the ER roofboards compared with those of the LMR/ScR. (BRB Residuary)

Sunday 12 August

61395 (38E Woodford Halse) seen on York shed after working in from Leicester on either the 10.0 p.m. (216) or the 10.12 p.m. (376) ex-Marylebone, Saturday 11th.

Saturday 18 August

60016 *Silver King* works throughout between Edinburgh and York, non-stop through Newcastle, unusually, probably on the 9.50 p.m. ex-Waverley (eleven coaches of 363 tons inc. BSK).

Saturday 25 August

Combined train 216 (eleven coaches of 363 tons inc. cafeteria car) runs from Marylebone departing at 10.0 p.m. to Newcastle, arriving at 5.25 a.m. then Waverley at 7.58/8.12 a.m. and Queen St (LL) at 9.45 a.m.

Friday 21 September

45677 *Beatty* takes last-of-season Up Starlight out of St Enoch.

Saturday 29 September

Last Down east coast service is train 365 M'bone, dep. 9.45 p.m. Waverley arr. 7.15 a.m. Formed of seven coaches of 231 tons inc. cafeteria car.

Financial Results

| From | Trains | | Tickets | | Receipts |
	Out	Rtn	Adult	Child	£
St Pancras	42	43	12,158	2,027	49,393
Marylebone	35	37	10,038	1,622	40,684
St Enoch	62	63	23,438	2,669	94,173
Waverley	41	43	13,540	1,832	55,630
Total 1956	180	186	59,174	8,150	239,880
Total 1955	185	189	64,535	8,640	240,994
Total 1954	196	204	73,793	9,118	274,232

Receipts in 1956	£239,880
Deduct refunds on unused tickets	11,000
Deduct operating costs	180,000
Estimated net profit	48,880

Receipts accruing to the Hotel & Catering Service from the supply of light refreshments in trains for the twenty-one weeks to 18 August 1956 were £10,570.

As seen from the table above, total passenger numbers were again down on the previous year. Various contributory causes were advanced for this; bad weather, changes in travel habits evidenced by the growth of private motoring, less money available in certain areas for travel – probably due to a curtailment of overtime working in some industries.

Average train loadings were similar to those of last year, however, and it was not considered that the increase of 5s in the return fare had had any effect on passenger numbers, as the coach fare had also been increased.

It was also noted by the commercial committee that the independent company Northern Roadways Ltd had surrendered its licence to operate their Edinburgh to London service and a group of tours starting from Edinburgh. All the pre-booked passengers on these Anglo-Scottish services were being conveyed by Scottish Omnibuses Ltd (BTC-owned), who had also asked for additional duplicates on their Edinburgh/London route and had applied to take over the group of tours from Edinburgh. There had been no change in the activity of Northern Roadways so far as their Glasgow to London route was concerned.

The 1957 Season

This commenced, as was now customary, with a northbound departure from London on Maundy Thursday – 18 April – with this stock forming the first southbound train from Scotland next day, Friday 19 April. The last outward departure was to be on Friday 20 September with the season's final return Starlight working on Saturday 5 October. The adult return fare was also raised to 80s.

In the early part of the season (i.e. the opening seven weekends) combined trains from/to Glasgow and Edinburgh were again run, as follows:

Down trains

M193		M193	
Thursday 18 April		Saturdays April 27, May 4/11/18/25, June 1/8	
Friday 26 April, May 3/10/17/24/31		(NB Rep. No. 370 on 26/27 April only)	
St Pancras dep. 11.0 p.m.		St Pancras dep. 10.40 p.m.	
Trent	1.27 a.m.	Trent	1.30 a.m.
Masborough	2.34/2.44 a.m. W	Masborough	2.10/2.17 a.m. W
(SouthSidings)		(South Sidings)	
Wath Rd Jct	2.57 a.m.	Newcastle	5.20 a.m.
Newcastle	5.38 a.m.	Waverley	7.32/7.55 a.m.
Waverley	7.58/8/10 a.m.	Queen St (HL)	9.12 a.m. (first three Sundays)
St Enoch	9.28 a.m.	St Enoch	9.21 a.m. (other Sundays)

Up trains

(446)		(447)	
Fridays April 19/26, May 3/10/17/24/31		Saturdays April 20/27, May 4/11/18/25, June 1	
St Enoch dep. 8.0 p.m.		St Enoch dep. 8.00 p.m.	
Waverley	9.25/9.40 p.m.	Waverley	9.25/9.40 p.m.
Newcastle	12.0 a.m.	Newcastle	11.56 p.m.
Rotherham	2.36/2.45 a.m. W	St Pancras	7.20 a.m. (Sun) May 4/11
(Masboro')			6.50 a.m. May 18/25
Trent	3.51 a.m.		
Leicester	4.16/4.24 a.m. K	W = loco water stop	
St Pancras	6.40 a.m. (Saturday)	K = stop for replenishment of cafeteria car	

Throughout this period eleven-coach sets of former LMS stock were used, formation being BSK/4SK/caf car/4SK/BSK of 345 tons tare, though on Friday 26 April train 446 was made up of twelve cars of 372 tons. Only for trains 370 on Saturday 27 April and trains M193/447/M193 on Friday 24/Saturday 25 May was a rake of ex-LNER vehicles used, same eleven-coach formation, weighing 363 tons.

After these opening weeks, separate Edinburgh trains again began running to/from Marylebone, the following being typical timings for the parent trains:

Up trains

Friday 14 June (446)		Saturday 15 June (447)
Waverley dep.	9.40 p.m.	9.40 p.m.
Newcastle	12.0 a.m.	11.56 p.m.
Marylebone	6.56 a.m. (Saturday)	6.56 a.m. (Sun)

Down trains

Friday 14 June (370)		Saturday 15 June (370)
Marylebone dep.	9.40 p.m.	9.40 p.m.
Newcastle	4.36 a.m.	4.53 a.m.
Waverley	6.57 a.m. (Saturday)	7.16 a.m. (Sun)

These were of ER stock, eleven coaches (inc. cafeteria car) totalling 363 tons tare.

The direct St Pancras–St Enoch specials reverted to running via Leeds and the S&C line, typical timings being (according to the Working Timetable 17/6 to 15/9/57).

Fridays (M183)			Fridays (M195)	
St Pancras dep.	8.50 p.m.		St Pancras dep.	11.20 p.m.
Nottingham	11.22/11.26 p.m. W		Trent	1.54 a.m.
Sheffield (M)	12.36/12.45 a.m. W		Masboro' (SS)	3.0/3.6 a.m. W
Whitehall Jct	1.57/2.7 a.m. L		Whitehall Jct	4.6/4.16 a.m. L
Hellifield	3.0/3.5 a.m. W			
Carlisle	4.47/4.58 a.m. K		L = loco change	

M183 to run every Friday to 6 September conditional 21 June and 6 September.

M195 definite 28 June–30 August

Saturday (M193)

St Pancras dep.	10.40 p.m.	Whitehall Jct dep.	3.13/3.23 a.m. L
Trent dep.	1.3 a.m.	Carlisle dep.	5.55/6.5 a.m. K
Masboro' dep. (SS)	2.10/2.17 a.m. W		

These trains run definitely 29 June to 31 August and conditionally 22 June and 7 September.

E 4   WEEKDAYS   LEEDS TO CARLISLE   LEEDS TO CARLISL

DOWN		B	C	C	A	A	A	A	G		A	A	B	G	A	A	A	B	A
		9.55 pm Pcls. from Derby Park Sidings	Pcls to Leeds City South	11.10 pm Nottingham to Edinburgh		8.50 pm London St. Pancras to Glasgow St. Enoch	9.0 pm St. Pancras to Edinburgh	9.0 pm St. Pancras to Edinburgh	2.25 am LE Leeds City South to Leeds Central	9.15 pm St. Pancras to Glasgow	9.15 pm St. Pancras South to Rison		LE	3.52 am Leeds City South to Rison	11.0 pm St. Pancras to Glasgow			11.20 pm St. Pancras to Glasgow
		P461			181	183	185	185		191	191			193					195
		SX	MX	MX	SO	SO	SX	SO			SO	SX		MO		SO			SO
		am	am	am	am	am	am ⬥	am ⬥	am		am ⬥	am	am	am	am	am ⬥	am	am	am ⬥
LEEDS CITY NTH.. dep	1			1 45			2 10	2 10			2 54	3 4	3 10			4 0			
Leeds City Jn.	2			1*47			2 26				3 53								
Whitehall Jn.	3		1 20		1L54 SL	2L 7 SL	2X27 FL	FL			1X54 FL	FL		3L58		SL 4L16			
Holbeck Low Level	4		SL								3 55			4 3					
... dep	5										4 0			4 6					
Wortley Jn.	6			1X22 FL				2*33			4 1								
Armley Canal Road	7																		
Kirkstall	8																		
Newlay and Horsforth	9																		
Calverley and Rodley	10																		
Apperley Jn.	11																		
Apperley Bridge and R.	12																		
Guiseley Jn.	13																		
Shipley Leeds Jn.	14				2 8	2 22	2 25	2 30			3 9	3 19				4 15			4 31
BRADFORD F.S.. dep	15	2 0														4 20			
Manningham	16																		
Frizinghall	17																		
SHIPLEY	18	2 5											3 27			4 22	4 25		
... dep	19	2 6	1 38										3 32			4 34			
Frizinghall	20																		
Manningham	21												3 39			4 41			
BRADFORD F.S.. arr	22		1 46																
Saltaire	23																		
Bingley	24																		
KEIGHLEY arr	25	2 19				2 16	2 30	2 33	2 38		3 18	3 28				4 26			
...	26	2 21									3 25	3 35							4 40
Steeton and Silsden	27																		
Kildwick and Crosshills	28																		
Cononley	29																		
SKIPTON arr	30	2 34			2L27	2 40	2 44	2 49			3 36	3 46				4 39			4 51
... dep	31				2W32		2 51	2 56											
Gargrave	32																		
Bell Busk	33																		
HELLIFIELD arr	34					3 0	3 7	3 12											
Long Preston	35				2 53	3 5	3 10	3 15			3 50	4 0				4 55			5 8
Settle Jn.	36																		
	37				3 0	3 10	3 15	3 20			3 54	4 4				5 0			5 13
Giggleswick	38																		
Clapham	39																		
... dep	40																		
Bentham arr	41																		
... dep	42																		
Wennington arr	43																		
... dep	44																		
Arkholme	45																		
Borwick	46																		
CARNFORTH arr	47																		
Hornby	48																		
Caton	49																		
Halton	50																		
Lancaster Green Ayre arr	51																		
... dep	52										4||p53	4||p53		5p||30					
Lancaster Castle.. dep	53										5* 3	5* 3		5* 5					
MORECAMBE P. arr	54										5* 5	5* 5							
... dep	55										5||15	5||15		5||50					
HEYSHAM arr	56																		
Settle	57																		
Horton	58																		
Ribblehead	59																		
Blea Moor	60				3 22	3 32	3 37	3 42			4 16	4 26				5 28			5 46
Dent	61																		
Garsdale arr	62																		
... dep	63																		
Hawes	64																		
Ais Gill	65				3 35	3 45	3 50	3 55			4 29	4 39				5 45			6 6
Kirkby Stephen West	66																		
APPLEBY WEST arr	67					4 8	4 13												
... dep	68				3 52	4 2	4 10	4 15			4 46	4 56				6 5			6 16
Long Marton	69																		
New Biggin	70																		
Culgaith	71																		
Langwathby	72																		
Little Salkeld	73																		
Lazonby and Kirkoswald	74																		
Armathwaite	75																		
Cumwhinton	76																		
CARLISLE arr	77				4 31	4 47	4 50	4|59			5 19	5 30				6 45			7 19

Extracts from working timetables valid from 17 June to 15 September 1957, giving details of some of the West Coast 'Starlight' timings. Page E4 – see columns 183, 193, 195. Page E22 – see cols 193, 195. Pages E44/45 and D28 – see columns headed 4, 6. (BRB Residuary)

E 22   ///// **SUNDAYS** /////   **LEEDS TO CARLISLE**

DOWN	No.	B	C		C	B	A	A	A	A	G	G	A	G	C
		11.15 pm (Sat) from Blackburn	12.2 am Pcls Leeds City South to Leeds Central		9.55 pm Pcls from Derby		9.0 pm St. Pancras to Edinburgh	9.15 pm St. Pancras to Glasgow	News to Huddersfield	10.40 pm St. Pancras to Glasgow	5.25 am LE from Carnforth Loco.	LE	10.50 pm St. Pancras to Glasgow	5.45 am from Carnforth Loco.	Pcls
					P461		185	191	193				195		P497
		am	am		am	am	am	am	am	am	am	am	am	am	am
LEEDS CITY NTH.. dep	1						2 10	2 54	3 14						
Leeds City Jn.	2		12 3												
Whitehall Jn.	3		12X 4 (SL/FL)		SL 1L20		FL	FL	3 16	3L23			3L38		
Holbeck Low Level arr	4														
dep	5														
Wortley Jn.	6		12 6		1X22 FL					*Whitehall Jn. arr 3L13 am*			*Whitehall Jn. arr 3L28 am*		
Armley Canal Road	7														
Kirkstall	8														
Newlay and Horsforth	9														
Calverley and Rodley	10														
Apperley Jn.	11														
Apperley Bridge and R.	12														
Guiseley Jn.	13				*Leeds E.S. Jn. 1.15*										
Shipley Leeds Jn.	14						2 25	3 9		3 38			3 53		
BRADFORD F.S. dep	15					2 0									4 45
Manningham	16														
Frizinghall	17														
SHIPLEY arr	18					2 5									
dep	19				1 38	2 6							[4]		4 51
Frizinghall	20														
Manningham	21														
BRADFORD F.S. arr	22				1 46										
Saltaire	23														
Bingley	24														
KEIGHLEY arr	25						2 19		3 18				[12]		5 0
dep	26						2 21	2 33	3 25	3 47			4 2		5 6
Steeton and Silsden	27														
Kildwick and Crosshills	28														
Cononley	29														
SKIPTON arr	30						2 34	2 44							5 19
dep	31						2 51		3 36	3 58			4 13		5 25
Gargrave	32														
Bell Busk	33														
HELLIFIELD arr	34	12 2					3 7								5L42
dep	35						3 10	3 50		4 13			4 32		5L44
Long Preston	36														
Settle Jn.	37						3 15	3 54		4 17			4 36		5 49
Giggleswick	38														
Clapham arr	39														
dep	40														
Bentham arr	41														
dep	42														
Wennington arr	43														
dep	44														
Arkholme	45														
Borwick	46														
CARNFORTH arr	47														
Hornby	48														
Caton	49														
Halton	50														
Lancaster Green Ayre arr	51														
dep	52								5 29			5‖p40			
Lancaster Castle arr	53														
MORECAMBE P. arr	54								5 37			5‖42		6° 2	
dep	55								5 42					6° 5	
HEYSHAM arr	56								5 55			6‖3		6‖15	
Settle	57														
Horton	58														
Ribblehead	59														
Blea Moor	60						3 37	4 16		4 42			5 1		6 14
Dent	61														
Garsdale arr	62														
dep	63														
Hawes	64														
Ais Gill	65						3 50	4 29		4 56			5 17		6 28
Kirkby Stephen West	66														
APPLEBY WEST arr	67						4 8								6 48
dep	68						4 10	4 46	5 14				5 35		7 12
Long Marton	69														
New Biggin	70														
Culgaith	71														
Langwathby	72														
Little Salkeld	73														
Lazonby and Kirkoswald	74														
Armathwaite	75						[6]								
Cumwhinton	76														
CARLISLE arr	77						4 50	5 19		5 55			6 20		7 48

Vertical notes shown in the table:
- col 185/191 (rows 6–13): *Limited Load*
- col 193 (rows 57–): *Not advertised* ; *Moss Sidings arr 5.48, dep 5.50*
- col P461 (rows 38–47): *Maximum Loading. Class 4F 410 tons, Class 5 425 tons, Class ... 460 tons*
- col 195 (rows 19–): *Leeds and Hellifield* ; *Ais Gill and Carlisle*
- "From 30th June to 8th September inclusive" ; "From 7th July to 1st September inclusive"
- "Via Western Division" ; "Not advertised"
- col 10.40 Glasgow: *To work 6.30 am Morecambe to Euston* ; *To work 6.30 am Morecambe to Leeds City Nth.*
- *To work 7.0 am Heysham to Morecambe*
- col 185 (rows 72–76): *Appleby and Carlisle*
- Keighley: *Whitehall Jn. arr 1L18 am. Sets down Guard*

E 44 WEEKDAYS — CARLISLE TO LEEDS — WEEKDAYS E 45

UP		B	G	G	G	G	C	C	G	G	G	A	A	G	A	A	A	A	A
		To Ilkley	LE to Carnforth Loco.	LE	LE	Fols to Sheffield	ECS Morecambe Euston Road		LE	LE	Two LE	8.0 pm Glasgow to St. Pancras	8.0 pm Glasgow to St. Pancras	LE to Carnforth Loco.	8.35 pm to St. Pancras	8.35 pm Glasgow to St. Pancras	8.55 pm Glasgow to St. Pancras	9.5 pm Glasgow to St. Pancras	9.5 pm Glasgow to St. Pancras
						P496						4	4		6	6	8	10	10
		SX AT PM	SO PM	SX PM	SX PM	SO PM	PM 10 55	FO PM	SO PM	SO PM	SX PM	FO PM 11 10	SO PM 11 10	SO PM	FO PM 11 30	SO PM 11 30	FO PM 11 43	FSX PM 11‡57	FO PM 11‡57
CARLISLE .. .. dep	1																		
Cumwhinton	2																		
Armathwaite	3																		
Lazonby and Kirkoswald	4					11 19													
Little Salkeld	5											11 36	11 36		11 56	11 56	12 7	12 18	12 20	12 20
Langwathby	6																		
Culgaith	7																		
New Biggin	8																1—11.56	1—11.56	
Long Marton	9																	1—11.56	
APPLEBY WEST .. arr	10											Not advertised	Not advertised		Not advertised	Not advertised			
.. dep	11						11 39					11 59	11 59		12 17	12 17	12 30	12 38	12 40	12 40
Kirkby Stephen West ..	12						12 11					12 32	12 32		12 48	12 48	1 0	1 6	1 10	1 10
Ais Gill	13																		
Hawes .. dep	14																		
Garsdale .. arr	15																		
.. dep	16																		
Dent	17											12 46	12 46		1 1	1 1	1 13	1 18	1 23	1 23
Blea Moor	18																		
Ribblehead	19					12 25													
Horton	20																		
Settle	21																		
HEYSHAM .. dep	22						11‖15	11‖25		11‖35									
MORECAMBE P. .. arr	23			11‖5	11‖35		11‖45			11‖49				11‖50					
Lancaster Castle .. dep	24		11‖0	11‖18	11*49		11*30		11‖40	11*49									
Lancaster Green Ayre dep	25		11‖p12		11‖p25	11‖p59			11‖p45	11‖p50 12*									
Halton	26																		
Caton	27																		
Hornby	28																		
CARNFORTH .. dep	31																		
Borwick	32																		
Arkholme	33																		
Wennington .. arr	34											12 22							
.. dep	35																		
Bentham .. arr	36																		
.. dep	37																		
Clapham .. arr	38											12 37							
.. dep	39																		
Giggleswick	40																		
Settle Jn.	41					12 38						12 52	12 59	12 59		1 14	1 14	1 26	1 31	1 36	1 36
Long Preston	42																		
HELLIFIELD .. arr	43					12L43						11‖p0							
.. dep	44					12L45							1 5	1 5		1 18	1 18	1 30	1 34	1 40	1 40
Bell Busk	45																		
Gargrave	46																		
SKIPTON .. arr	47					1 2													
.. dep	48					1 16						1 21	1 21		1 31	1 31	1 43	1 46	1 53	1 53
Cononley	49																		
Kildwick and Crosshills	50																		
Steeton and Silsden	51																		
KEIGHLEY .. arr	52					1 28						1 34	1 34		1 43	1 43	1 54	1 56	2 3	2 3
.. dep	53																		
Bingley	54																		
Saltaire	55																		
BRADFORD F.S. dep	56	10 20																	
Manningham	57	10 23																	
Frizinghall	58	10 26																	
SHIPLEY .. arr	59	10 28																	
Frizinghall .. dep	60	10 29																	
Manningham	61																		
BRADFORD F.S. arr	62																		
	63																		
Shipley Leeds Jn.	64					1X36						1 42	1 42		1 52	1 52	2X 3	2X14	2X14
Guiseley Jn.	65					FL						SL	SL		SL	SL	SL	FL	FL	FL
Apperley Bridge and R.	66																		
Apperley Jn.	67																		
Calverley and Rodley	68																		
Newlay and Horsforth	69																		
Kirkstall	70																		
Armley Canal Road	71																		
Wortley Jn.	72																		
Holbeck Low Level .. arr	73																		
.. dep	74																		
Whitehall Jn.	75											1 54	1 54		2 8	2 8				
Leeds City Jn.	76																		
LEEDS CITY NTH. arr	77					1 52									2 18	2 20	2‡32	2 34	

D 28   WEEKDAYS   LEEDS TO TRENT   LEEDS TO TRI[ENT]

UP

Mileage					Station	No.	C	C	C	A	A	C	A	A	A	A	C	C
							Fish to Birmingham	Fish to Birmingham	Pcls to Bedford	1.25 am Manchester L Rd to Cleethorpes	8.0 pm Glasgow to St. Pancras	10.55 pm Glasgow to Carlisle	2.8 pm from York	8.35 pm Glasgow (FO) to St. Pancras	9.5 pm Glasgow to St. Pancras	8.35 pm Glasgow (FO) to St. Pancras	10.55 pm Pcls from Carlisle	10.55 pm Pcls from Carlisle
M	C	M	C	M	C			P485	P485	P452	4		P496	6	10	8		P496	P496
								MSX	SO	MX		SO♦		SO	SX	SO		SO	SX
								am	am	am	am	am	am	am	am	am	am	am	am
0	0					LEEDS CITY NTH. dep	1			12 25		2 8			2 31	2 28			2 34
0	56					Leeds Engine Shed Jn.	2				2L6				2L22				
1	67					Hunslet	3												
5	79					Woodlesford	4												
7	53					Methley North	5												
8	44					Methley Jn.	6												
9	47					Altofts and Whitwood	7												
10	1					Altofts Jn.	8			12 44	2 22	2 29	2 37		2 43	2 46	2 50		2 54
10	70					NORMANTON arr	9			12 46	2K40								
						dep	10			12 59	2 24 TL	2 32 TL		2 45 TL	2 48	2 52 TL		2 57 TL
14	67	0	0			Walton	11												
		8	13			Thornhill Midland Jn.	12												
17	53					Royston Jn.	13												
18	54					Royston and Notton	14												
						Royston Loco. dep	15												
20	6			0	0	Cudworth North Jn.	16												
				3	47	BARNSLEY C.H. arr	17				2 24								
20	43	0	0	0	0	Cudworth South Jn. dep	18				2 27								
20	73	3	47	3	77	Cudworth South Jn.	19												
						CUDWORTH arr	20				2 52 SL						2 52 SL		3 17
		6	58	2	23	Monk Spring Jn. dep	21			1 19	2 42	3 15→		3 3	3 7	3 10		3 15	3 27
		4	5			Wombwell West	22			1 26									3 24
		5	51			Elsecar and Hoyland	23												
		7	6			Wentworth	24												
		8	53			Chapeltown South	25			1 39									3 40
		10	6			Ecclesfield West	26												
24	53					Darfield	28												
26	75					Wath North	29												
28	8					Wath Road Jn.	30				2 54			3 15	3 19	3 24			3 40
28	72					Swinton Town	31												
30	5					Kilnhurst West	32												
32	3					Parkgate and Rawmarsh	33												
34	1	0	0			ROTHERHAM MAS. arr	34												
34	39					Holmes dep	35				3 0			3 22	3 26	3 30			3 48
36	6					Wincobank	36												
36	18					Wincobank Station Jn.	37												
36	49	12	70			Brightside	38						1 45						3 50
38	43					Attercliffe Road	39												
39	37					SHEFFIELD MID. arr	41						1 51		3 34	3 38		3 57	3 57
40	68					Heeley dep	42	1 32 FL	1 32 FL	2 20 FL					3 41 FL	3 47 FL			
41	22					Heeley Carriage Sidings	44												
42	16					Millhouses and Ecclesall	45												
43	3					Beauchief	46												
43	58					Dore and Totley arr	47												
						dep	48	1 43	1 43	2 31					3 52	3 58			
46	34					Dronfield	49	1 48	1 48	2 36					3 57	4 3			
48	10					Unstone Colliery Sidings	50												
50	1	0	36			Sheepbridge	51												
		1	11			Masboro' South Jn.	52												
						Masboro' S.S. arr	53								3W3	3W25			
		6	32			dep	54								3W12	3W34			
		12	17			Beighton Jn.	55								3 25	3 47			
51	58	15	59			Barrow Hill	56												
						CHESTERFIELD M. arr	57				2 42				3 58	4 2			4 8
53	63					Hasland dep	58	1 53	1 53	2 52	3 36				3 58	4 2			4 8
55	59					Clay Cross	60	1 58	1 58	2 58	3 41				4 3	4 7			4 13
58	74					Morton Sidings	61	2 4		3 4	3 46				4 9	4 13			4 18
59	27					Doe Hill	62												
60	69					Westhouses and Blackwell	63												
61	75					Alfreton and S. Normanton	64												
64	40					Pye Bridge	65	2 16		3 16	3 58				4 21	4 25			4 30
65	32					Codnor Park and Ironville	66												
68	8					Langley Mill and Eastwood	67												
71	26					Ilkeston Jn. and Cossall	68												
72	64	0	0			Trowell	69				3 29				4 10	4 33	4 37		4 42
		5	7			Radford	70												
		7	22			NOTTINGHAM arr	71												
74	6					Stanton Gate	72												
75	29					Stapleford and Sandiacre	73												
77	19					Long Eaton	74												
77	42					North Erewash Jn.	75												
78	13					TRENT arr	76				3 40				4 17		4 41	4 44	4 49

The two basic trains out of St Pancras were the parent train at 11.0 p.m. (M193, Saturdays also) and 'Q' train at 11.20 p.m. (M195). These were backed up when required by earlier trains leaving at 8.50 p.m. (Fridays M183), 9.0 p.m. (Saturdays M185) and 9.15 p.m. (M191, Fridays & Saturdays). All had ten- or eleven-minute stops at Carlisle to change crews and replenish cafeteria car supplies.

Southbound, the parent and 'Q' trains out of St Enoch left at 8.0 p.m. (M4, Fridays and Saturday s) and 8.35 p.m. (M6, Fridays and Saturday s) respectively, again with ten-minute stops at Carlisle (11.0–11.10 p.m. for M4, 11.20–11.30 p.m., for M6) for Holbeck men to take over from Corkerhill footplate staff. Again, these trains were supplemented by extra portions as demand required.

At the height of the season, some Starlights were also scheduled to start in the Glasgow district and north of Edinburgh, to serve local holiday patterns, for example:

Friday 5 July

445 Waverley 7.12 p.m.	Newcastle 9.43 p.m.	Marylebone 5.18 a.m.
446	8.35 p.m.	11.18 p.m.	6.40 a.m.
447 Aberdeen 4.25 p.m.	Waverley 8.38/8.53 p.m.	7.8 a.m.
448 Waverley 9.5 p.m.	Newcastle 11.39 p.m.	7.25 a.m.
213 Aberdeen 4.45 p.m.	Waverley 9.8/9.23 p.m.	7.31 a.m.

Notes

- The Aberdeen trains picked up at several intermediate points before reaching Edinburgh.
- It would appear that no cafeteria cars were available for these excursions (against stated provision), all five 11-coach trains having refreshments served from a central BSK.

Departures from Edinburgh the following week were similar.

Friday 12 July

445/447/448 started from Waverley with the same timings to Marylebone as on the 5th, plus:

446		213	
Cardenden dep. 6.35 p.m.		Kirkcaldy dep. 8.10 p.m.	
Waverley	8.15/8.35 p.m.	Waverley	9.8/9.23 p.m.
Marylebone	6.40 a.m. (Saturday)	Marylebone	8.0 a.m. (Saturday)

Notes

- In both cases the trains also served other Fifeshire stations on the way to Edinburgh
- Return trains ran Saturday 27 July (K'caldy 9.20 a.m., C'den 11.16 a.m.)
- Only train 448 was equipped with a cafeteria car (as opposed to a minimum of two), BSKs again being used on the four others.

Saturday 13 July
The maximum number of Starlights depart Marylebone (6) on return workings, as follows.

	214	216	376	377	378	379
Marylebone dep.	9.40 p.m.	9.55 p.m.	10.8 p.m.	10.50 p.m.	11.30 p.m.	11.45 p.m.
Waverley dep.	7.16 a.m.	7.46 a.m.	8.0 a.m.	8.40 a.m.	9.29 a.m.	9.45 a.m.

Friday 19 July
Trains 446/448 operate as on 5 July, plus the following:

213		447	
Dundee (Tay Bridge) dep. 7.10 p.m.		Dundee (TB) dep. 6.35 p.m.	
Waverley	9.8/9.23 p.m.	Waverley	8.33/8.53 p.m.
Marylebone	7.31 a.m. (Saturday)	Marylebone	7.8 a.m. (Saturday)

Note: Again extra stops were made between Dundee and Edinburgh.

Euston again saw several trains arrive from St Enoch at peak times, as follows:

Friday 26 July
W534, W536 both St Enoch–Euston, while W535 ran Kilmarnock–Euston (all three fourteen cars of 435 tons)

and in the reverse direction:

Saturday 27 July
W697 Euston dep. 10.22 p.m.
W691 Euston dep. 11.5 p.m., calling at Hamilton, Motherwell
W695 Euston dep. 11.55 p.m. Hamilton, M'well, Coatbridge
W701 Euston dep. 12.20 a.m. (Sun), calling at Cartairs, M'well
W701 had caf car, others BSK. All fourteen cars of 435 tons.

and on the Midland route the maximum number of Starlights left for St Enoch on:

Friday 26 July
M583/4/5/6/7/8 all departed St Pancras (though M585 went to Glasgow Central). All twelve cars of 372 tons.

F12 WEEKDAYS MARYLEBONE TO WOODFORD HALSE WEEKDAYS F13																	
DOWN		B	B	A	A	C	A	A	A	G	B	B	A	G	G	B	B
				To Edinburgh ✶	To Edinburgh ✶	Parcels to Preston	To Edinburgh ✶	To Manchester London Rd. and Liverpool Cent.	To Manchester London Rd. and Liverpool Cent.	2 L.E.'s to Neasden Loco			To Manchester London Rd. and Liverpool Central	L.E. to Kensington	L.E. to Kensington		
		418	422	214	214	250	216	54	54	300	428	428	54	184	184	434	434
			SO	FO HC ♠	SO HC ♠	FSX	FSOQ HC ♠	SX	FOQ	SX		Q	SO	THO	TO	SX	SO
		PM	PM	PM	PM	PM	PM	PM	PM	PM	PM	PM	PM	PM	PM	PM	PM
MARYLEBONE .. .. dep	1	9 20	9 32	9 40	9 40	9 45	9 55	10 0	10 0	10‖10	10 20	10 20	10 45	..	..	11 20	11 20
Marylebone Goods ...... dep	2																
Neasden Loco	3	..	..	..	..	..	..	[1]	[1]	..	..	..	[1]	11‖15	11‖15	..	..
Neasden South Jn. ...... arr	4									10 21							
.. .. dep	5	9 29	9 41	9 50	9 51	9 57	10 6	10 10	10 10	10 22	10 29	10 29	10 55	11 18	11 18	11 29	11 29
Neasden Sidings	6																
Wembley Hill	7	..	..	..	..	..	..	..	..	..	10 33	10 33	..	..	..	..	..
Sudbury and Harrow Road ..	8	PL			PL	PL	PL				PL	PL		PL	PL	PL	PL
Sudbury Hill (Harrow)	9	PL	..	..	PL	PL	PL	..	..	..	PL	PL	..	PL	PL	PL	PL
Northolt Park	10										10 41	10 41					
Northolt Jn. East	11	9 39	..	...	10 4	10 8	10 19	..	..	..	10 44	..	..	11 30	11 30	11 39	11 39
South Ruislip	12											10 45					
Ruislip Gardens	13	..	..	..	..	..	..	..	..	..	..	..	..	..	..	..	..
West Ruislip	14	9 43									10 48	10 49		11▽24	11▽24	11 43	11 43
Denham	15	9 48	..	..	..	..	..	..	..	..	10 53	10 54	..	..	..	11 48	11 48
Denham Golf Club	16	9 51									10 56	10 57				11 51	11 51
Gerrards Cross	17	9 56	..	..	..	..	..	..	..	..	11 1	11 2	..	..	..	11 56	11 56
Seer Green	18	10 1½									11 6½	11 7½				12 1½	12 1½
Beaconsfield	19	10 5½	..	..	..	..	..	..	..	..	11 10½	11 11½	..	..	..	12 5½	12 5½
HIGH WYCOMBE .. arr	20	10 12½									[2] 11 20	[2] 11 21				[2] 12 15	12 12½
.. dep	21	10 15	..	..	10 25	10 30	10 40	..	..	..	..	..	..	..	..	..	12 15
West Wycombe	22																
Saunderton	23	..	..	..	..	..	..	..	..	..	..	..	..	..	..	..	[3]
PRINCES arr	24	10 28															12 31
RISBOROUGH dep	25	10 31	..	..	10 38	10 41	10 53	..	..	..	..	..	..	..	..	..	..
Monks Risborough	26	10 35															
Little Kimble	27	10 39	..	..	..	..	..	..	..	..	..	..	..	..	..	..	..
South Aylesbury	28																
Haddenham	29	..	..	..	..	..	..	..	..	..	..	..	..	..	..	..	..
Ashendon Jn.	30				10 49	10 54	11 4										
HARROW-ON- arr	31	..	9 46	..	..	..	..	..	..	..	..	..	..	..		..	..
THE-HILL dep	32		9 47	9 55				10 15	10 15				11 0				
North Harrow	33	..	9 51	..	..	..	..	..	..	..	..	..	..	..		..	..
Pinner	34		9 54														
Northwood Hills	35	..	9 58	..	..	..	..	..	..	..	..	..	[1]	..		..	..
Northwood	36		10a 2½														
Moor Park	37	..	10 6	..	..	..	..	..	..	..	..	..	..	..		..	..
Watford South Jn.	38		10 8	10 4				10 24	10 24				11 8				
RICKMANSWORTH arr	39	..	10 10	..	..	..	..	..	..	..	..	..	..	..		..	..
dep	40		10 11	10 6				10 26	10 26				11 10				
Chorley Wood	41	..	10 18	..	..	..	..	..	..	..	..	..	..	..		..	..
Chalfont	42		10 24	10 15				10 33½	10 33½				11 17				
Chesham .. .. arr	43	..	..	..	..	..	..	..	..	..	..	..	..	..		..	..
Amersham	44		10 30														
Great Missenden .... arr	45	..	..	..	..	..	..	..	..	..	..	..	..	..		..	..
...... dep	46		10 38	10 24				10 42	10 42				11 25				
Wendover	47	..	10 46	[3]	..	..	..	[3]	[3]	..	..	..	[3]	..		..	..
Stoke Mandeville	48		10 51														
AYLESBURY arr	49	10 48	10 56	..	..	..	..	10 56	10 56	..	..	..	11 38	..		..	..
TOWN dep	50		11 5	10 36				11 6	11 6				11 46				
Quainton Road	51	..	11c16	10 43	..	..	..	11 14	11 14	..	..	..	11 53½	..		..	..
Grendon Underwood Jn.	52		11 21	10 48	10 57	11 3	11 12	11 16½	11 17½				11 56				
Calvert	53	..	11c26	..	..	..	..	..	..	..	..	..	..	..		..	..
Calvert North Jn.	54					11 7			[4]				[2]				
Claydon L.N.E. Jn.	55	..	..	..	..	11*27	..	..	..	..	..	..	..	..	..	..	..
Finmere	56		11c36														
Brackley .. .. arr	57	..	11 45	..	..	..	..	11 30	11 33	..	..	..	12 11	..	..	..	..
.... dep	58							11 32	11 35				12 13				
Helmdon	59	..	..	..	..	..	..	[3]	..	..	..	..	..	..	..	..	..
Culworth	60												[2]				
Culworth Jn.	61	..	..	11 9	11 18	..	11 33	11 44½	11 44½	..	..	..	12 23	..	..	..	..
WOODFORD arr	62							11 48	11 48				12 26				
HALSE dep	63	..	..	11 11	11 20	..	11 35	11 50	11 50	..	..	..	12 28	..	..	..	..
				[2] Quainton Road and Grendon Underwood Jn.		Claydon L.N.E. Jn. arr. 11*11 worked by E.R. to Bletchley No. 1 arr. 11L53.		Runs in FOQ times when 216 runs.	Applies when 216 FOQ runs.	Neasden Loco arr. 10‖25 Passenger Pilots		To operate for special events at Wembley on dates to be circularised.		To work 10.35 p.m. Dover Marine to Newcastle	Runs 18th June, 2nd and 23rd July, 6th and 27th August. Q Other Tuesdays. To work 10.35 p.m. Dover Marine to Newcastle.		

Extracts from working timetables valid from 17 June to 15 September 1957, giving details of some of the East Coast 'Starlight' timings. Pages F12 and F26 – see columns 214, 216. Pages F30, F44 – see columns 213, 215. (BRB Residuary)

F26 WEEKDAYS — BANBURY TO SHEFFIELD — WEEKDAYS F27

DOWN	No.	C	B	A	A	C	A	A	A	A	A	A	A
		E.C.S. to Mansfield		7.33 p.m. from Swindon	7.33 p.m. from Swindon	8.50 p.m. Parcels Marylebone Gds. to York	9.40 p.m. Marylebone to Edinburgh	9.40 p.m. Marylebone to Edinburgh	9.55 p.m. Marylebone to Edinburgh	9.55 p.m. Marylebone to Edinburgh	10.0 p.m. Marylebone to Manchester and Liverpool	10.0 p.m. Marylebone to Manchester and Liverpool	9.40 p.m. Swindon to York
		365	354	160	160	128	214	214	216	216	54	54	208
		FO	FX	FSX	FSO	SX	FO HC ♠	SO HC ♠	SOQ HC ♠	FOQ HC ♠	SX	FO Q	SX
		PM	PM	PM	PM	PM	PM	PM	PM	PM	PM	PM	PM
BANBURY arr	1			9 4	9 4								11 35
GENERAL dep	2			9 16	9 16								11 50
Banbury Jn	3			9 19	9 19								11 53
Culworth Jn	4			9 29	9 29	10 44	11 9	11 18	11 33	11 33	11 44½	11 44½	12 4
WOODFORD arr	5			9 32	9 32						11 48	11 48	12 8
HALSE dep	6			9 37	9 37	10 46	11 11	11 20	11 35	11 35	11 50	11 50	12‡15
Charwelton	7			[3]	[3]		[2]	[3]	[3]	[3]		[3]	
Braunston & Willoughby	8												
RUGBY CENTRAL arr	9			9 58	9 58						12 7½	12 10½	12 31
dep	10			10 3	10 3	11 4	11 28	11 38	11 53	11 53	12 12½	12 15½	12 35
Lutterworth	11				10c16								
Ashby Magna	12			[3]	[3]		[2]	[3]	[3]	[3]	[3]	[3]	[5]
Whetstone	13												
LEICESTER CENTRAL arr	14			10 29	10 35	11L30	11L50½	12L1½	12L16½	12L16½	12 37	12 40	1 1
dep	15		10 20	10 42	10 45	11L36	11L56½	12L7½	12L22½	12L22½	12 47	12 50	1 11
Belgrave and Birstall	16		10 25										
Rothley	17		10 31										[1]
Quorn and Woodhouse	18		10 37										
LOUGHBOROUGH arr	19		10 41	10 56	10 59						1 0½	1 3½	1 26
CENTRAL dep	20		10 42	10 58	11 1	11 51	12 8½	12 19½	12 34½	12 34½	1 4½	1 7½	1 28
East Leake	21												
Rushcliffe Halt	22												
Ruddington	23												
Arkwright Street	24												
NOTTINGHAM arr	25		11 5	11 17	11 20	12 10					1 22	1 25	1 49
VICTORIA dep	26	10†55		11 32	11 32	12 27	12 23	12 34	12 49	12 49	1 37	1 40	2 4
New Basford	27												
Bagthorpe Jn.	28	11 1		11 37	11 37	12 33	12 27	12 38	12 53	12 53	1 42½	1 45½	2 10
Bulwell Common	29					12 35							
Hucknall Central	30			11 45	11 45								
Annesley South Jn.	31	11 12				12 44							[1]
Annesley Loco	32												
Hollinwell and Annesley	33												
Kirkby South Jn.	34	11 15		11 53	11 53	12 48	12 42	12 53	1 8	1 8	1 57½	2 0½	2 25
Kirkby Bentinck	35												
Tibshelf Town	36												
Pilsley	37												
Heath arr	38												
dep	39												
Heath Jn.	40			12 7	12 7		12 56	1 7	1 22	1 22	2 11½	2 14½	2 39
CHESTERFIELD arr	41												
CENTRAL dep	42												
Staveley Works	43												[1]
STAVELEY CENTRAL arr	44												
dep	45			12 15	12 15		1 4	1 15	1 30	1 30	2 19½	2 22½	2 47
Renishaw Central	46												
Killamarsh Central	47												
Killamarsh Jn.	48									[1]			[2]
Waleswood Jn.	49												
Woodhouse East Jn.	50			12 23	12 23		1 12	1 23	1 38	1 39	2 27½	2 30½	2 57
Woodhouse	51			[3]	[3]		[6]	[3]	[3]	[3]	[3]	[3]	[3]
Darnall	52						1 33	1 41	1 56	1 57			
Attercliffe Jn.	53						1 36	1 44	1 59	2 0			
Blast Lane arr	54												
dep	55												
SHEFFIELD arr	56			12 34	12 34						2◇40	2◇43	3 8
VICTORIA dep	57										2‡50	2‡53	3 40
		To form 11.50 p.m. to Nottingham Victoria. From 12th July to 6th September inclusive.					Orgreaves GL arr. 1▽17 dep. 1W23 ML	Orgreaves GL arr. 1▽28 dep. 1W34 ML	Orgreaves GL arr. 1▽34 dep. 1W49 ML	Orgreaves GL arr. 1▽44 dep. 1W50 ML		Applies when 216 FOQ runs	‡12.10

F30 WEEKDAYS — SHEFFIELD TO BANBURY

UP

M	C	M	C	Station	No.	A	A	G	G	C	A	A	G	C		C	G	B	B
						6.38 p.m. Glasgow to Marylebone	9.40 p.m. Newcastle to Bournemouth Cen.	3.25 a.m. L.E. from Colwick	L.E.	E.C.S.	9.23 p.m. Edinburgh to Marylebone	9.40 p.m. Edinburgh to Marylebone	L.E.	E.C.S.		E.C.S.	L.E.	Staff	
						217	211	166	315	255	213	215	2017	305		291	180	2021	303
						MWFO HX ♠	SO	SO	MX		SOQ HC ♠	SO HC ♠		SX			SO		SX
						am	am	am	am	am	am	am	am	am		am	am	am	am
0	0			SHEFFIELD .. arr	1	..	..	..	..	..	..	..	..	..	..	..	..	..	..
				VICTORIA .. dep	2														
		0	0	Attercliffe Jn.	3	..	1 37	..	..	..	3 5	3 19	..	..	..	..	..	..	..
1	74	0	52	*Darnall*	4		1 40				3 8	3 22							
4	70			Woodhouse	5	..	[1]	..	..	..	..	..	..	..	..	..	..	..	..
5	24			Woodhouse East Jn.	6		1 47				3 28	3 40							
		0	0	Waleswood Jn.	7	..	..	..	..	..	..	..	..	..	..	..	..	..	..
7	39	1	66	Killamarsh Jn.	8														
8	15			Killamarsh Central	9	..	..	..	..	..	..	..	..	..	..	..	..	..	..
9	74			Renishaw Central	10														
11	79			STAVELEY CENTRAL arr	11	..	..	..	..	..	..	..	..	..	..	..	..	..	..
		0	0	dep	12		1 56				3 37	3 49				2 Sets. To form 6.0 a.m. SO, 6.20 a.m. SX to Marylebone and 8.0 a.m. to Leicester Central.			
		1	60	Staveley Works	13	..	..	..	..	..	..	..	..	..	..		..	..	..
		5	8	CHESTERFIELD arr	14														
				CENTRAL dep	15	..	..	..	..	..	..	..	..	..	..		..	..	..
17	41	9	65	Heath Jn.	16	..	2 7	..	..	2 sets E.C.S. To form 7.38 a.m. to Rugby Central and 6.0 a.m. to Sheffield	3 48	4 0	..	..	..		..	..	..
17	67			Heath arr	17														
				dep	18	..	..	..	..		..	..	..	..	..		..	..	..
20	19			Pilsley	19														
21	52			Tibshelf Town	20	..	..	..	..		..	..	..	..	..		..	..	..
26	35			Kirkby Bentinck	21														
27	27			*Kirkby South Jn.*	22	2 26	2 21	..	..		4 2	4 14	..	..	..		..	..	..
28	47			Hollinwell and A.	23													6 10	
		0	0	Annesley Loco	24	..	..	..	..		..	..	4‖35	..	..		5‖15	..	..
29	48	0	28	Annesley South Jn.	25								4 40				5 20	6 12	
32	27			Hucknall Central	26	..	..	..	..		..	..	..	..	..		..	6 18	..
34	67			Bulwell Common	27								4‖50				5Z32	6 23	
35	79			Bagthorpe Jn.	28	2 36	2 30	..	..		4 11	4 23	..	..	..		..	..	..
36	43			New Basford	29					4† 5						4†58			
38	10			NOTTINGHAM arr	30	2▽41	2 35½	3 38	..	4†10	..	..	..	..	..	5 †3	..	..	..
				VICTORIA dep	31	2▽43	2 41	3 45			4 15	4 27					5 40		
39	0			*Arkwright St.*	32	..	..	..	..	..	..	..	..	..	..	..	5‖45	..	..
42	40			Ruddington	33														
46	13			Rushcliffe Halt	34	..	..	..	..	..	..	..	..	..	..	..	..	..	..
47	10			East Leake	35														
51	54			LOUGHBOROUGH arr	36	..	2 59½	..	..	..	..	..	..	..	..	..	..	..	..
				CENTRAL dep	37	2 59½	3 2	4 5			4 30½	4 42½							
53	58			Quorn and Woodhouse	38	..	..	..	..	..	..	..	..	..	..	..	..	..	..
56	43			Rothley	39	[3]	[3]				[3]	[3]							
59	19			Belgrave and Birstall	40	..	..	..	..	..	..	..	..	..	..	..	..	..	..
61	45			LEICESTER CENTRAL arr	41	3W13	3 18	4‖20			4L45	4L57				B			
				dep	42	3W20	3 23	..	..	..	4L52	5 L 4	..	5†45	..	To Marylebone	..	..	6 20
66	22			Whetstone	43														6 29
70	61			Ashby Magna	44	[3]	[3]	..	..	..	..	..	..	B	..		..	..	6 39
74	52			Lutterworth	45														6 48
81	35			RUGBY CENTRAL .. arr	46	..	3 51	..	..	..	..	..	..	6†25	..		..	..	6 58
				dep	47	3 45	3 53				5 15½	5 27½							7 5
86	9			Braunston and W.	48	..	..	..	..	..	..	..	..	..	..		..	..	..
93	13			Charwelton	49	[3]	[3]				[3]	[3]							
95	47			WOODFORD arr	50	..	..	..	..	..	..	..	..	..	..	251	..	..	7 25
				HALSE dep	51	4 4	4 14		5‖30		5 35	5 47				6 23			
97	27			*Culworth Jn.*	52	4 6	4 16	..	5 35	..	5 37	5 49	..	..	..	6 27	..	..	..
105	44			Banbury Jn.	53		4 29		5 51										
106	57			BANBURY GENERAL arr	54	..	4 32	..	5‖55	..	..	..	..	..	..	..	..	..	..
				dep	55		4 40												
							From 13th July to 24th August inclusive. [2] Culworth Jn. and Banbury Jn.	To work 5.20 a.m. to Llandudno. From 6th July to 7th September inclusive	To work 6.50 a.m. Parcels to Sheffield		GL Rotherwood arr. 3▽16 a.m., dep. 3W24 a.m. ML	GL Rotherwood arr. 3▽30 a.m., dep. 3W36 a.m. ML	To work 5.30 a.m. to Hollinwell	To form 7.35 a.m. to Leicester			To work 6†15 a.m. to Tibshelf Town. From 6th July to 31st August inclusive. Z—To pick up guard.	Not advertised	

Starlight Specials

F44 WEEKDAYS   WOODFORD HALSE TO MARYLEBONE

UP	G	C	B	G	C	B	C	G	B	A	B	A	C	G
	5.0 a.m. LE from Kensington	2.35 a.m. Parcels from Leicester London Rd.		L.E.	Parcels		E.C.S.	L.E.	9.23 p.m. from Edinburgh			9.40 a.m. from Edinburgh	5.45 a.m. Parcels from Bletchley	L.E.
	245	235	307	238	309	313	329	248	315	213	315	215	545	24
	SO	MX			MX	SX	SX	SO	SO	SOQ HC ↓	SX	SO HC ↓	MX	
	am	am	am	am	am	am	am	am	am	am	am	am	am	am
WOODFORD HALSE arr (1)														
dep (2)														
Culworth Jn. (3)										5 35		5 47		
Culworth (4)										5 37		5 49		
Helmdon (5)														
Brackley arr (6)														
dep (7)														
Finmere (8)														
Claydon L.N.E. Jn. (9)		4 52												6 8
Calvert North Jn. (10)		4 54												6 10
Calvert (11)														
Grendon Underwood Jn. (12)		4 57								5 56		6 8		6 14
Quainton Road (13)														6 17
AYLESBURY TOWN arr (14)														6 25
dep (15)				••••			6†10							
Stoke Mandeville (16)				••		5 1								
Wendover (17)						5 20								
Great Missenden arr (18)						5 29								
dep (19)						5 35								
Amersham (20)						5g48								
Chesham dep (21)			5 38											
Chalfont (22)			5 47			5g56								
Chorley Wood (23)			5 51			6c2								
RICKMANSWORTH arr (24)			5 56			6 7								
dep (25)			5 57			6 10								
Watford South Jn. (26)			5 59			6 12								
Moor Park (27)							f.							
Northwood (28)			6a 4			6c18								
Northwood Hills (29)			6 7											
Pinner (30)			6 11			6c25								
North Harrow (31)			6 14											
HARROW-ON-THE-HILL arr (32)			6 18			6 32								
dep (33)			6 19			6 37				[2]		[5]		
Ashendon Jn. (34)		5 4								6 6		6 21		
Haddenham (35)														
South Aylesbury (36)														
Little Kimble (37)														
Monks Risborough (38)														
PRINCES RISBOROUGH arr (39)							6†25							
dep (40)		5 19								6 18		6 33		
Saunderton (41)														
West Wycombe (42)														
HIGH WYCOMBE arr (43)														
dep (44)		5 33				5 55				6 15	6 30	6 25	6 45	
Beaconsfield (45)						6 3½				6 23½		6 33½	6 47	
Seer Green (46)						6 7½				6 27½		6 37½		
Gerrards Cross (47)						6 13				6 33		6 43		
Denham Golf Club (48)						6 17				6 37		6 47		
Denham (49)			PL			6 20				6 40	[7]	6 50		
West Ruislip (50)	5*37					6 25				6 45		6 55		
Ruislip Gardens (51)						6 28				6 48		6 58		
South Ruislip (52)						6 31				6 51		7 1		
Northolt Jn. East (53)	5 45	5 56								7 0		7 8		
Northolt Park (54)						6 35				6 55		7 5		
Sudbury Hill (Harrow) (55)	PL	PL				6 38				6 58		7 8		
Sudbury and Harrow Road (56)	PL	PL				6 41				7 1		7 11		
Wembley Hill (57)						6 45				7 5		7 15		
Neasden Sidings (58)														
Neasden Loco (59)				6‖30				7 0						7‖18
Neasden South Jn. arr (60)				6 33				7 3						7 22
dep (61)	6 0		6 6	6 24	6 34	6 43	6 48	7 4		7 8	7 14	7 18	7 20	7 23
Neasden Loco arr (62)	6‖4				[3]		[3]			[3]	[3]	[3]	[3]	
Marylebone Goods arr (63)		6 20												
MARYLEBONE arr (64)			6 35	6‖45	6 52	6 59		7‖15		7 19	7 25	7 29	7 31	7‖34

At the end of the season, a combined Glasgow/Edinburgh train left on:

Friday 20 September (446)
St Enoch dep. 8.0 p.m., Wav'y 9.23/9.40 p.m., N'castle 12.0 a.m., M'bone 6.40 a.m.

This returned (M193) on Saturday 5 October as:
St Pancras dep. 10.40 p.m. (BST)
Newcastle   4.3 a.m. (GMT)
Waverley   6.28/6.40 a.m.
Queen St (HL)   7.53 a.m. (Sun)

In between, Saturday 28 September saw the interesting working of train 447 departing Waverley at 9.40 p.m. reaching Newcastle at 12.4 a.m. and King's Cross at 5.52 a.m.

Marylebone was unavailable as the recently introduced 'car sleeper' was due in at (more or less) the Starlight arrival time.

Financial Results

From	Trains		Tickets		Receipts
	Out	Rtn	Adult	Child	£
St Pancras	42	43	11,878	1,986	51,584
Marylebone	27	28	7,669	1,232	33,140
Glasgow	57	56	20,590	2,472	87,454
Edinburgh	39	41	12,631	1,735	56,066
Totals 1957	165	168	52,768	7,425	228,244
Totals 1956	180	186	59,174	8,150	239,880
Totals 1955	185	189	64,535	8,640	240,994

	£
Receipts	228,244
Deduct refunds on unused tickets	12,500
Deduct operating costs	170,305
Estimated net profit	45,439

Receipts accruing to the Hotel & Catering services from the supply of light refreshments on trains for the eighteen weeks to 17 August 1957 were £8,891.

Note: 'Glasgow' and 'Edinburgh' includes fares for Starlight Specials starting back at other points in Scotland.

It was noteworthy that the early part of the season was particularly well patronised and the latter part very poorly. In the first twelve weeks to 6 July, sixty trains ran (thirty-eight in 1956), an increase of 58 per cent, and there were 10,000 extra passengers, an increase of 104 per cent. (Though the latter included the Edinburgh Trades Holiday

Friday 3 May. Platform 1 at St Enoch with 60094 *Colorado* waiting to leave on the 8.0 p.m. to St Pancras, via Waverley. (W. A. C. Smith/Transport Treasury)

Saturday 29 June. M4, the 8.0 p.m. 'parent' train from St Enoch to St Pancras, awaits departure time in platform 1 behind 46117 *Welsh Guardsman*, which will take the train through to Leeds (Whitehall Junction). Note that the LMS stock is now in the 1956 lined maroon livery. (Brian Morrison)

traffic; the 1957 season began three weeks later than 1956 because Easter was later.)

In the first sixteen weeks to 3 August, 120 trains ran (ninety-three in 1956), an increase of 29 per cent and there were an extra 12,000 passengers, an increase of 37 per cent.

However, at this time (3 August) advance bookings were 13,400 down (56 per cent decrease) and the number of trains required were forty-three (seventy-five in 1956) i.e. 43 per cent down.

It was also mooted that, as a heavy proportion of costs was represented by coaching stock, this might be reduced if the stock could be used for other purposes during the week. It was therefore agreed that the commercial and operating departments should jointly explore the possibility of running some Starlight Specials mid-week, which would both increase stock utilisation and ease the pressure on coaching stock at peak weekends.

This proposal was duly examined by these departments. Both bodies concluded that any diversion of these excursion trains to mid-week was undesirable (for various reasons) and that, apart from peak periods when it was already the practise to utilise Starlight stock as circumstances allow, there was in general no stock shortage.

Observations and workings throughout the season

1. Friday 19 April, 60812 leaves St Enoch with the 8.0 p.m. combined train for St Pancras via Edinburgh, running ECS to Waverley. 45697 *Achilles* + 45573 *Newfoundland* head the 8.35 p.m. direct train to St Pancras via Barrhead, as far as Leeds.

2. Friday 26 Apr 60933 takes the combined train out of St Enoch at 8.00 p.m.

3. Friday 3 May 60094 *Colorado* takes the combined train from St Enoch at 8.00 p.m.

4. Friday 17 May 60043 *Brown Jack* takes the combined train from St Enoch at 8.00 p.m.

5. Saturday 29 June 46117 *Welsh Guardsman* heads train M4 (8.0 p.m. St Enoch to St Pancras) between Glasgow and Leeds.

6. Friday 12 July 8 Starlights leave St Enoch with Glasgow Fair traffic. 60035 *Windsor Lad* heads train 446 (6.35 p.m. from Cardenden) between Waverley and York.

7. Saturday 13 July 60907/60929/60954/60977 all serviced at 34E (Neasden) having worked south on Glasgow Fair traffic which originated at Edinburgh. 73158 (34E) works to York with a Down Starlight, and is then used on trains to Hull, Harrogate! 61842 (38E Woodford Halse) arrives in York off another Down special, and then works to Scarborough!

8. Saturday 20 July 61472 (50A York) reaches Marylebone on one of the two trains from Dundee (Tay Bridge).

9. Saturday 3 August 61306 (53B Hull Botanic Gardens) works into St Pancras (from Leeds?) with an Up Starlight. The first B1 here since the 1948 Interchange Trials!

STARLIGHT SPECIAL
TO LONDON

From Edinburgh (Waverley) and Glasgow (St. Enoch)

Every Friday night
From 19th April to 20th September, 1957

80/-   Return Fare
Second Class.
Children Half-Fare.   **80/-**

Stay 8 or 15 days.   Fare includes reserved seat.   Express night travel.
Night buffet available.

ADVANCE BOOKING ESSENTIAL

Booking opens on Thursday, 3rd January, for all Fridays except Edinburgh Trades Holiday Friday (28th June) and Glasgow Fair Friday (12th July.) Booking for these two dates opens on Thursday, 10th January.

Full details at Stations and Agencies.

Starlight Special trains will also be run from the undernoted places on the Friday night immediately preceding the local annual holidays:—

Aberdeen	Dunfermline	Kilmarnock
Cardenden	Galashiels	Kirkcaldy
Clydebank	Gourock	Lochgelly
Coatbridge	Greenock	Motherwell
Cowdenbeath	Hamilton	Paisley
Dumbarton	Hawick	Port Glasgow
Dundee	Inverkeithing	Stonehaven

Details of fares and train times and the opening dates for booking from these places will be announced later.

BRITISH RAILWAYS

A British Rail advertisement for the 1957 season complete with a list of additional starting points in Scotland to suit local holidays. Advance bookings opened in London on Tuesday 1 January. (BRB Residuary)

The 1958 Season

Pre-season general arrangements

Fares were again increased this year, the adult return going up to 85s, and advanced bookings began on Wednesday 1 January in England, Thursday 2 January in Scotland. The season was to commence as usual with northbound departures from London on Maundy Thursday 3 April, this stock forming the first southbound combined train on Good Friday, 4 April. The last outward excursions were scheduled for Friday 19 September with the final return working on Saturday 4 October.

  After Easter, early season trains were again combined services and timings were to be

M193	St Pancras dep.	10.40 p.m.	446	St Enoch dep.	8.0 p.m.
	Waverley	7.57/8.10 a.m.		Waverley	9.23/9.40 p.m.
	Queen St (HL)	9.26 a.m.		St Pancras	6.45 a.m.

Eleven coaches of 363 tons (inc. caf car)   Eleven coaches of 345 tons (inc. caf car)

Combined trains were scheduled St Pancras to Edinburgh/Glasgow as follows:

Outwards: Fridays 11 April–16 May inclusive
Return: Saturday 12 April–17 May inclusive

and in the reverse direction:

Outwards: Fridays 4 April–30 May plus 19 September
Return: Saturday 12 April–7 June plus 4 October

Compartment stock to be provided on all combined trains, plus cafeteria car.

Trains to be provided, outbound
Ex-St Pancras: maximum of four departures on any one night.

Ex-St Enoch, as above except on:

    4 July, seven trains: three to St Pancras, four to Euston
    18 July, nine trains: six to St Pancras, three to Euston
    1 August, seven trains: four to St Pancras, three to Euston

All these west coast excursions to be formed of compartment stock, except:

    4 July, one train from Glasgow
    18 July, four trains from Glasgow (Glasgow Fair Holiday)
    1 August, one train from Glasgow

Ex-Marylebone: one 'parent' train and one 'Q' train, winter timetable. Maximum of four departures during summer timetable.
Ex-Waverley: as above except on 18 July when there were five trains to Marylebone

All 'parent' and 'Q' trains on the east coast route to be formed of compartment stock. Additional services to be of open stock.

Despite the above provision, bookings from London for the Easter holiday were insufficient to warrant the running of independent trains from St Pancras and Marylebone, so that last-minute arrangements were made to run a combined train instead. (Combined trains also had to be run from St Pancras on 23 May and 12 and 19 September instead of independent trains.)

For successive weeks between Easter and Whitsuntide even the combined trains laid down could not be justified, and Starlight Special passengers, again at short notice, had to be carried by ordinary services from both London and Scotland, though this was not a desirable arrangement.

With such a slow start to the season, and with a considerable decrease in advance bookings evident, the Scottish Region introduced a system of deferred payments. Under this scheme a passenger paid £1 deposit (per person) at the time of application, with the balance not less than fourteen days prior to the date of travel. This method began on 14 April and by 2 May 1,233 bookings had been made. Despite this, in the first five weeks of operation only three Starlights had actually run as scheduled (eight ran in the first five weeks of the 1957 season) due to lack of support for trains originating in both London and Scotland. These were therefore cancelled and passengers conveyed by ordinary services. Suggested reasons for the lower than expected response were the reduction in spending power and the fact that the facility had lost some of its original novelty. As a result, bookings (actual and advance) were down by 25 per cent after ten weeks.

The working timetable valid 9 June–14 September gives the following timings for the two cafeteria car-equipped Starlights on the west coast route. Unless otherwise stated, all St Pancras–St Enoch trains had the formation: BSK/4SK/RCAF/5SK/BSK of twelve coaches of 370 tons.

RCAF indicated restaurant cafeteria car, though the exterior branding just said cafeteria, and it would not be offering restaurant facilities anyway.

Down trains

Fridays M193		M195 (Q)		definite 4 July to
St Pancras dep.	11.0 p.m.	11.20 p.m.		29 Aug; Q 13, 20,
Leicester	1.1 a.m. (Sat)	1.27 a.m.		27 June and 5 Sept
Trent	1.27 a.m.	1.54 a.m.		
Masboro'	2.34/2.42 a.m. (W)	3.0/3.6 a.m. (W)		
South Sidings				
Wath Rd Jct	2.54 a.m.	3.16 a.m.		
Cudworth	3.8 a.m.	3.28 a.m.		

Saturdays M193		M195 (Q)		definite 28 June to
St Pancras dep.	10.40 p.m.	10.50 p.m.		30 Aug; Q 14 June
Leicester	12.39 a.m. (Sun)	12.50 p.m.		and 13 Sept
Trent	1.3 a.m.	1.19 a.m.		
Masboro'		2.9/2.16 a.m. (W)	2.24/2.31 a.m. (W)	
Wath Rd Jct	2.26 a.m.	2.41 a.m.		
Cudworth	2.38 a.m.	2.53 a.m.		

Up trains

Fridays M4		M6 (Q)	Friday to 16 Aug
St Enoch dep.	8.0 p.m.	8.35 p.m.	and 30 Aug
Cudworth	2.42 a.m. (Sat)	3.3 a.m.	
Masboro'	3.4/3.13 a.m. (W)	3.26/3.35 a.m. (W)	
Trent	4.17 a.m.	4.41 a.m.	Saturdays definite from
Leicester	4.43 a.m.	5.8 a.m.	13 July onwards
St Pancras	6.50 a.m.	7.12 a.m.	Q 22/29 June, 6 July

(Saturday timings for M4, M6 were the same as Fridays)

On the east coast route, after the outbound trains on Friday 6 June had returned eight or fifteen days later, there was a lull in operations until the Edinburgh and Fifeshire holidays.

At this time, five specials left Edinburgh as follows:

Friday 4 July

445	Waverley	7.7 p.m.	Marylebone	5.15 a.m. (BSK)
446	Waverley	8.35 p.m.	Marylebone	6.40 a.m. (BSK)
447	Waverley	8.53 p.m.	Marylebone	6.56 a.m. (BSK)
448	Waverley	9.5 p.m.	Marylebone	7.10 a.m. (BSK)
213	Waverley	9.23 p.m.	Marylebone	7.25 a.m. (cafeteria car)

All eleven-coach trains of 363 tons with 213 as 'parent' train. The following week, on Friday 11 July, 213 starts back at Aberdeen departing at 4.45 p.m., then as above, and on Friday 18 July 447/448 ran as above, plus:

446   213
Cardenden dep. 6.35 p.m.   Kirkcaldy dep. 8.10 p.m.
Waverley   8.15/8.35 p.m.   Waverley   9.7/9.23 p.m.
Marylebone   6.40 a.m.   Marylebone   8.0 a.m.

and in the reverse direction   216
                                           Marylebone dep. 9.55 p.m.
                                            Waverley   7.52 a.m.

Friday 18 July was also Glasgow Fair Friday, and the whole of the traffic offering from Glasgow on this day could not be accommodated and the overflow was conveyed in three further trains on Saturday 19th, the first time that Saturday had been used as a departure date since 1955. For details of the eleven Starlights departing Glasgow see the accompanying duplicated publicity material. (Note that the Euston trains were appreciably 'quicker'!)

STARLIGHT SPECIALS

For the information of passengers holding Starlight tickets, details of the Starlight Special Trains which will run from Glasgow to London on Glasgow Fair Friday, 18th July and Saturday, 19th July, are as follows:—

Leave	Arrive		Train coaches labelled
GLASGOW (St. Enoch)	**LONDON** (St. Pancras)	**LONDON** (Euston)	
18th July p.m.	19th July a.m.	19th July a.m.	
3 40	3 5	—	J
6 15	5 32	—	H
7 0	—	4 20	E
7 10	6 3	—	C
7 45	6 45	—	D
8 0	6 52	—	A
8 35	7 12	—	B
9 55	—	7 30	F
19th July p.m.	20th July a.m.	20th July a.m.	
7 10	6 2	—	K
7 45	6 38	—	L
10 20	—	7 50	M

Only passengers holding Starlight Rail tickets can join these trains and passengers must join the train labelled to correspond with the departure time, coach label and the seat number shewn on their tickets.

Passengers return from London by Special Starlight train on Saturday, 26th July, or Saturday, 2nd .... number shewn on their Starlight Ticket.

As all seats on the Starlight Special Trains are reserved, passengers in possession of Starlight tickets need not present themselves at the departure station more than half an hour before the departure time stated on their tickets.

(BRB Residuary)

Friday 25 July

216 ran as above (18th) 447 starts Dundee (TB) dep. 6.13 p.m. (BSK) and also C 605 Galashiels dep. 8.5 p.m.

Hawick	8.34/8.45 p.m.
Carlisle	10.0/10.10 p.m. reaching St Pancras at 6.3 a.m.

Two west coast Down trains also ran to St Enoch, as under (both twelve coaches of 372 tons)

M585	St Pancras dep. 11.40 p.m.	M586	St Pancras dep. 12.0 midnight
	Carlisle 8.10/8.18 a.m.		Carlisle 8.49/8.55 a.m.

plus W 533   St Enoch–Euston formation BSO/6SO/BSK/5SO/BSO
Carlisle 9.37/9.45 p.m.   fourteen coaches of 435 tons
Crewe 12.56 a.m. (K)   K = stop for replenishing refreshments

Friday 1 August

Another busy night!

C603	St Enoch–St Pancras	C605 Paisley (Canal) – St Pancras
	Carlisle 9.2/9.10 p.m.	Carlisle 10.0/10.10 p.m.

C606   Paisley (Gilmour St) – St Pancras M585 St Pancras dep. 11.40 p.m.
Carlisle 10.14/10.22 p.m.   Carlisle   8.10/8.18 a.m.

All four trains were of twelve coaches, all take water and change crews at Carlisle, plus:

W534	W535	W536
Kilmarnock – Euston	St Enoch–Euston	St Enoch–Euston
Carlisle 10.45/10.55 p.m.	12.39/12.52 a.m. (Saturday)	1.8/1.15 a.m. (Saturday)
Preston 12.51 a.m. (Saturday)	2.51 a.m.	3.17 a.m.
Crewe 1.59 a.m. (L)	4.5 a.m. (K)	4.28 a.m. (K)

All three trains fourteen coaches, formation as W533 above.

Returning Glasgow Fair Holiday traffic predictably produced the largest number of Down trains possible, ten in total, six from St Pancras and four from Euston.

Saturday 2 August

M583	St Pancras– St Enoch	Carlisle 6.57/7.5 a.m. (K)
M584	Glasgow (C)	7.15/7.23 a.m. (K)
M585	Glasgow (C)	7.32/7.40 a.m. (K)
M586	St Enoch	8.8/8.16 a.m. (K)
M587	St Enoch	8.37/8.45 a.m. (K)
M588	St Enoch	9.9/9.16 a.m. (K)

All twelve-coach trains of 372 tons, two with cafeteria cars, four with BSKs, plus:

W687 Euston – Glasgow (Central)
     Crewe 1.40 a.m. (L) (Sun)
     Preston 2.50 a.m.
     Carlisle 5.25/5.35 a.m. (K)

W691 Euston–St Enoch
     2.20 a.m. (L)
     3.39 a.m.
     6.0/6.7 a.m. (K)

W693 Euston – Coatbridge
     Crewe 2.59 a.m. (L) (Sun)
     Preston 4.13 a.m.
     Carlisle 6.14/6.20 a.m. (K)

W701 Euston – Glasgow (Cen)
     3.32 a.m. (L)
     4.38 a.m.
     6.41/6.50 a.m. (K)

Reverting to east coast excursion traffic, Saturday 26 July 216 ran as above, plus 376 departing Marylebone at 10.8 p.m., Waverley departing at 8.0/8.20 a.m. and Aberdeen arriving at 12.15 p.m. (376: eleven coaches of 370 tons including RB.)

This route was again busy over the next weekend, as below:

Friday 1 August
215   Waverley dep. 9.40 p.m.   Marylebone 7.0 a.m.
216   Marylebone dep. 9.55 p.m.   Waverley 7.52 a.m.

Saturday 2 August
213   Waverley dep. 9.23 p.m.   Marylebone 7.25 a.m.
215   9.40 p.m.   7.0 a.m.
214   Marylebone dep.9.40 p.m.   Waverley   7.3 a.m.
376   10.8 p.m.   8.0 a.m.
          377   379
Marylebone dep. 10.50 p.m.   Marylebone dep. 11.45 p.m.
Waverley   8.25/8.40 a.m. Waverley   9.25/9.40 a.m.
Kirkcaldy   9.25 a.m.   Cardenden   11.0 a.m.

Further details of some of the above workings are revealed in the following document.

Newcastle Station Workings for Saturday 2 August (LE = light engine)

215   9.40 p.m. Waverley–Marylebone (Friday 1 August)
       arrive 12.3 a.m. depart 12.11 a.m. from platform 9, twelve coaches
       engine working; inbound – LE to Gateshead (duty Sc13)
       engine working; outbound – LE from Gateshead (duty Gd78)

214   9.40 p.m. Marylebone–Waverley (Friday 1 August)

Friday 4 July. 44786 + 45482 are seen near Cathcart West Junction with train C6 from Clydebank (Riverside) via Lugton to St Pancras. (W. A. C. Smith/Transport Treasury)

Friday 18 July. 40573 + a 'Jubilee' cross Strathbungo Junction with one of the many 'Starlights' to leave St Enoch. The train reporting number is on the second engine only. (W. A. C. Smith/Transport treasury)

arrive 5.6 a.m. depart 5.15 a.m. from platform 9
engine working inbound – LE tender-first to Scotswood Bridge Sidings (Y80)
engine working outbound – LE from Heaton (H3m)

216   9.55 p.m. Marylebone–Waverley (Friday 1 August)
arrive 5.18 a.m. depart 5.26 a.m. from platform 8
engine working; inbound – LE to Gateshead (G)
engine working; inbound outbound – LE from Gateshead (G)

213   9.23 p.m. Waverley–Marylebone
arrive 11.48 p.m. depart 11.56 p.m. from platform 9, 11 coaches
engine working; inbound – LE to Gateshead (Sc?)
engine working; outbound – LE from Gateshead, to work south

215   9.40 p.m. Waverley–Marylebone
arrive 11.59 p.m. depart 12.24 a.m. (Sunday 3 August) from platform 10
engine working; through from Edinburgh to York.
(BRB Residuary)

The following week saw, among others, two specials return to Dundee (Tay Bridge).

Saturday 16 August. It's 7.15 a.m. at Beaconsfield and 73169 is seen on the GW & GC Joint Line with an up train from Waverley. (John Chamney)

Saturday 9 August

		(both trains eleven coaches of 363 tons inc. BSK)	
376	M'bone 10.8 p.m.	Waverley 8.00/8.15 a.m.	Dundee 10.0 a.m.
377	M'bone 10.50 p.m.	Waverley 8.25/8.45 a.m.	Dundee 10.36 a.m.

Trains 213 and 216 dealt with the rest of the east coast traffic during August until the combined trains below (both twelve coaches of 372 tons inc. cafeteria car) took over.

M193	St Pancras 11.0 p.m.	Waverley 8.23/8.47 a.m.	St Enoch 9.59 a.m.
446	St Enoch 8.0 p.m.	Waverley 9.25/9.40 a.m.	St Pancras 6.40 a.m.

During the course of the peak period this season (six weekends), no less than thirty-six trains were provided with refreshments served from brake vans. While this had always been the case when more than two trains were running on any one night from any one terminal, it applied with particular force to the Scottish-originating traffic. (On no occasion did the number of Friday trains from Marylebone to Edinburgh exceed two, and on only one occasion did the Friday number from St Pancras to Glasgow exceed two). This has continually given rise to complaints in Scotland by the public and through the press, but with the introduction of new hygiene regulations, the Hotels & Catering Service (who staff these vehicles) stated they could not agree to the use of brake vans for the 1959 season. However, as no further cafeteria cars or buffet cars were available for Starlight trains, and in view of the fact that it would be a retrograde step to discontinue this facility on journey times of ten hours, the only option was to press the Hotels & Catering Services to repeat the usual arrangements with the proviso that the operating department ensure that the brake vans used were specially cleaned for the purpose.

Observations and workings throughout the season

1. Friday 4 April, 60959 heads first St Enoch–St Pancras, as far as Waverley.
2. Tue 29 April, 60094 *Colorado* brings Starlight ECS into Glasgow.
3. Thu 29 May, 60094 again brings ECS into Glasgow, from Crookston (first A3 noted on Canal Line).
4. Saturday 14 June, 92139 works roof-boarded ECS of 'Starlight Special' up Lickey, banked by 92079 and 8403. (East coast set of post-war LNER stock in maroon.)
5. Saturday 28 June, 45606 *Falkland Islands* brings W536 into Euston, with SC30018M as cafeteria car.
6. Friday 4 July, 72004 *Clan MacDonald* heads M524 from Gourock (fourteen coaches) through to Corkerhill where a pilot is attached to work to New Cumnock.
7. Friday 4 July, 44786 + 45482 depart Clydebank (Riverside) and run via Carmyle, Cathcart West Junction and Lugton.
8. Sunday 6 July, 45251 seen on Starlight stock, used for excursion traffic from Glasgow to the Clyde coast.
9. Friday 18 July, 40573 + 'Jubilee' noted at Strathbungo Junction.
10. Saturday 19 July, 70048 *The Territorial Army 1908–1958* enters Euston on W535 with SC670E as cafeteria car.

Friday 4 July. 72004 *Clan Macdonald* runs through Shields Junction with the fourteen-coach M524 from Gourock. On reaching Corkerhill a pilot will be attached for the climb to New Cumnock. (W. A. C. Smith/Transport Treasury)

11. Saturday 19 July, W536 from Coatbridge runs into Euston behind 46115 *Scots Guardsman*, having worked the train from Crewe.
12. Thursday 7 August, 92100 powers a Chesterfield–Ashburys excursion entirely composed of roof-boarded Starlight stock.
13. Friday 8 August, 92075 heads the same stock from Huddersfield to Sheffield (Victoria), which is working to Marylebone as a relief to the 'South Yorkshireman'.
14. Saturday 16 August, 73169 noted at Beaconsfield on an Up Starlight from Waverley.

Financial Results

From	Trains		Tickets		Receipts
	Out	Rtn	Adult	Child	£
St Pancras	26	26	8,367	1,416	38,569
Marylebone	20	21	5,495	969	25,438
Glasgow	49	52	18,375	2,058	82,641
Edinburgh	29	32	9,081	1,325	43,341
Totals 1958	124	131	41,318	5,768	189,989
Totals 1957	165	168	52,769	7,425	228,244
Totals 1956	180	186	59,174	8,150	239,880
Totals 1955	185	189	64,535	8,640	240,994
Totals 1954	196	204	73,793	9,118	274,232
Totals 1953	209	220	67,717	7,811	250,677

After allowing for costs, both operating and administrative, and also unused ticket refunds, it was estimated that the margin of profit for 1958 amounted to £40,189 compared with £45,439 for the 1957 season.

Receipts of £7,808 accrued to the Hotels & Catering Services, plus a further £8,000 or so on sales at refreshment rooms.

The fare for 1958 increased by 5s, following the general rise in rail fares in September 1957 and increases in the competitive road fares. No adverse criticism was received regarding this increase.

The following table shows the decline in the respective flows of Starlight traffic:

	Originating in England			Originating in Scotland		
	Passengers	Decrease	£	Passengers	Decrease	£
1953	30,266		99,378	45,262		150,939
1954	31,613	1,347 (inc.)	103,206	51,298	6,036 (inc.)	171,026
1955	27,124	4,489	88,040	46,051	5,247	152,954
1956	25,845	1,279	90,077	41,479	4,572	149,880
1957	22,765	3,080	84,724	37,428	4,051	143,520
1958	16,247	6,518	64,007	30,839	6,589	125,982

Although the reduction in traffic has been continuous (except in 1954), traffic was still substantial, and it was thought that a withdrawal or material change at this time in the facilities offered by the Starlight Specials would give rise to general disquiet.

When the annual results were compiled, increasing use of the private car for holiday purposes was added to the possible reasons for the further decline in total passenger numbers (and receipts), as was the counter-attraction of other holiday areas – including the Continent. Additionally, observation of the fact that post-Easter traffic had always been light until Whitsuntide – indeed five Starlights had to be cancelled this year through lack of support up to mid-May – led to the conclusion that the operating season was too long. Consequently, the decision was taken to discontinue the facility between Easter and Whitsuntide for 1959, when Good Friday fell on 27 March and Whit Sunday on 18 May. The 1959 season would also terminate one week earlier.

However, to mitigate the effect of rising costs, the operating department was asked to consider the possibility of concentrating all London traffic on Marylebone, and to improve the attraction of the service by the possibility of improving overall running times for these trains, as well as their punctuality. The desirability of extending the Starlight arrangement to other suitable points such as Blackpool or Scarborough was also to be examined, as was the question of retaining the Easter services, given that these were now to be isolated from the rest of the season.

Starlight Special

GLASGOW
and
EDINBURGH
to
LONDON

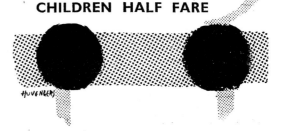

85/-
return

including reserved seats

CHILDREN HALF FARE

BOOK
NOW!

Friday 27th March and Fridays 15th May to 11th September

EXPRESS NIGHT TRAVEL · BUFFET

STAY 8 OR 15 DAYS · BOOK IN ADVANCE

FOR FULL DETAILS SEE OTHER SIDE

BRITISH RAILWAYS

★ **STARLIGHT SPECIAL TRAINS, one class only, will run on Friday nights** 27th March and 15th May to 11th September 1959, inclusive, from Glasgow to London and Edinburgh to London. Passengers will return by special trains from London on Saturday nights the 8th or 15th day after arrival.

★ **STARLIGHT SPECIAL TRAINS** assure seats to all passengers. Accommodation is limited and for this reason it is essential that passengers *BOOK IN ADVANCE STATING THE DATE ON WHICH THEY DESIRE TO TRAVEL FORWARD AND RETURN.*

★ **STARLIGHT SPECIAL TRAINS** are available only to holders of Starlight Special tickets specifying the appropriate train and date of travel.

★ **STARLIGHT SPECIAL TRAINS** run as shown below, and light refreshments are obtainable.

OUTWARD JOURNEY—FRIDAY NIGHTS

	27th March, 15th, 22nd and 29th May and 11th September	5th June to 4th September	5th June to 4th September
	p.m.	p.m.	p.m.
GLASGOW (St. Enoch)...leave	8 0	8 0	—
EDINBURGH (Waverley) ,,	9 40	—	9 40
	a.m.	a.m.	a.m.
LONDON (St. Pancras)..arrive	6 50	6 50	—
LONDON (Marylebone).. ,,	—	—	7 31

RETURN JOURNEY—SATURDAY NIGHTS

	4th and 11th April, 23rd and 30th May, 6th June and 26th September	13th June to 19th September	13th June to 19th September
	p.m.	p.m.	p.m.
LONDON (Marylebone)..leave	—	—	9 40
LONDON (St. Pancras)... ,,	10 40	10 40	—
	a.m.	a.m.	a.m.
EDINBURGH (Waverley)arrive	7 30	—	7 35
GLASGOW (St. Enoch) ... ,,	—	8 45	—
GLASGOW (Queen St.).. ,,	9 6	—	—

★ **STARLIGHT SPECIAL TRAIN TICKETS** are on sale at principal suburban stations and at Railway Ticket Agents in the Glasgow and Edinburgh areas. Remittances for the fare 85/- which includes a reserved seat in each direction (half fare for children aged 3 but under 14 years) must accompany all postal applications to:—

For Bookings from Glasgow:
Starlight Enquiry Office,
St. Enoch Station,
Glasgow.

Telephone No.: CITy 6128.

For Bookings from Edinburgh:
Starlight Enquiry Office,
Waverley Station,
Edinburgh.

Telephone No.: WAVerley 2477.
(Extension 444-5)

★ **STARLIGHT SPECIAL TICKETS ARE NOT TRANSFERABLE** and are issued subject to the bye-laws, regulations and conditions contained in the publications and notices of or applicable to the British Transport Commission. They are not available for break of journey. British Railways do not undertake to refund the value of lost, mislaid or unused tickets. Further information may be obtained on application to:

DISTRICT PASSENGER MANAGER, 50 George Square, Glasgow.

DISTRICT COMMERCIAL MANAGER, 23 Waterloo Place, Edinburgh.

TRAVEL LIGHT—SEND YOUR LUGGAGE IN ADVANCE

For passengers who prefer a Combined Road/Rail facility to London by ordinary services (out by road, return by rail or vice versa) tickets are obtainable at a fare of £5 from Scottish Omnibuses Ltd., 290 Buchanan Street, Glasgow, or 45 Princes Street, Edinburgh, who will supply details on request.

B.R. 35001—HN—January, 1959—B 25739.   McCorquodale, Glasgow.

(BRB Residuary)

The 1959 Season

As can be seen from the handbill, this year's fare remained at 85s adult return, but for the first time it was acknowledged that the early season excursions were not sufficiently popular to warrant running these *every* Friday. Hence the advertised break between the running of the Good Friday trains (27 March) and the start of the main season, which commenced on Friday 15 May, though the returning Saturday night trains did of course run on April 4/11. (Note that this is a ScR handbill; the first London departure was on Thursday 26 March, and no timings are therefore given for Friday night traffic originating at either St Pancras or Marylebone.)

The timings given in the handbill were for the 'parent' train only. If a Starlight ran in several parts, the schedule for this train may have differed slightly, though this of course was shown on the ticket itself.

The northbound returning Easter specials did not, in the event, adhere to the timings in the handbill – which was printed three months earlier and 'laid down' even sooner.

Saturday 4 April		*Saturday 11 April*	
M193		M193	
St Pancras dep.	10.40 p.m.	St Pancras dep.	10.40 p.m.
Waverley	8.7/8.17 a.m.	Waverley	7.45/7.54 a.m.
Queen St (HL)	9.31 a.m.	Queen St (HL)	9.10 a.m.
(eleven coaches of 363 tons)		(eleven coaches of 345 tons)	

The southbound return working on Saturday 11 April was as follows:

436
St Enoch dep. 7.45 p.m. Waverley 9.8/9.23 p.m. Marylebone 6.38 a.m.

This was a twelve-coach formation of 396 tons.

All Easter trains were of course combined Glasgow/Edinburgh services. Combined trains also carried the traffic booked for 15/22/29 May outward departures; thereafter from 5 June to 4 September separate trains ran between St Enoch and St Pancras

Friday 29 May. 60057 *Ormonde* is ready to depart from St Enoch's platform 2 with train 446, the 8.0 p.m. via Edinburgh to St Pancras. (W. A. C. Smith/Transport Treasury)

and between Waverley and Marylebone. The last outward Starlight of the season (11 September) and the final return working (26 September) were also combined trains.

As in previous years only the 'parent' train and first duplicate were guaranteed to include cafeteria cars (though even this didn't always happen last year!). All extra trains had refreshments available all night via a centrally located BSK.

Repeating the arrangement introduced last year, Scottish holidaymakers travelling to London could book in advance through a deferred payment scheme. By making a deposit of £1 per person, a seat each way was guaranteed and a voucher received. On payment of the balance (to be made not less than fourteen days before the outward journey), this voucher was then exchanged for a rail ticket.

Deferred payment facilities were also available at other Scottish centres from which Starlight Specials had been arranged to coincide with the local annual holidays. These were:

Aberdeen	Dunfermline	Kilmarnock
Cardenden	Galashiels	Kirkcaldy
Clydebank	Gourock	Lochgelly
Coatbridge	Greenock	Motherwell
Cowdenbeath	Hamilton	Paisley
Dumbarton	Hawick	Port Glasgow
Dundee	Inverkeithing	Stonehaven

The Starlight reservation offices at St Enoch and Waverley opened on Monday 12 January for all Fridays except Glasgow Fair (17 July) and Edinburgh Trades holiday (3 July). Bookings for these two dates commenced Monday 19 January.

Unfortunately, a national printing strike for two months caused the 'loss' of most of the details of this summer's interesting Starlight workings, only a few therefore being available, as below.

Friday 29 May
60057 *Ormonde* leaves St Enoch with the combined train to St Pancras, via Edinburgh.

Friday 10 July

	448	213
Waverley dep.	9.5 p.m.	9.23 p.m.
Newcastle	11.40/11.48 p.m. (L)	?
Dearn Jct	2.28 a.m. (Saturday)	?
Marylebone	7.10 a.m.	7.23 a.m.

Friday 17 July
Eight Starlight Specials depart St Enoch (Glasgow Fair) and one from Coatbridge/Motherwell/Hamilton.

Thursday 6 August
60918 (50A) works a set of roof-boarded Starlight ECS bound for Bradford, seen at Cleckheaton.

Saturday 8 August

	M976	M977
Marylebone dep.	10.10 p.m.	10.50 p.m.
Dearne Jct	2.44 a.m.	3.32 a.m.
York	3.28/3.35 a.m.	4.17/4.26 a.m.
Newcastle	5.19/5.29 a.m.	5.55/6.3 a.m.
Waverley	8.10 a.m.	8.40 a.m.
Dundee	?	?

These trains to be platformed at York and Newcastle for watering the cafeteria car, similarly:

444   Waverley dep. 8.35 p.m.
      Newcastle 11.15/11.23 p.m.
      York 1.20/1.37 a.m.
      Dearne Jct 2.14 a.m.
      Marylebone   ?

The final outward excursion and its return were both combined Glasgow/Edinburgh trains, scheduled as follows:

Friday 11 Sept 446		*Saturday 26 Sept* M193	
St Enoch dep.	8.0 p.m.	St Pancras dep.	10.40 p.m.
Waverley	9.26/9.40 p.m.	Waverley	8.19/8.30 a.m.
St Pancras	7.27 a.m.	Buchanan St	9.40 a.m.

Thus ending the season with an unusual use of an alternative Glasgow terminus. The opening train from St Enoch (on Friday 27 March) had also been unusual in its use of 60150 *Willbrook* (52A Gateshead) throughout from St Enoch to Newcastle.

As can be seen from the foregoing text for 1959, the suggestions made at the end of the 1958 season were not acted upon. Specifically, the use of one sole London terminus did not materialise (though it did in 1960) and the Blackpool/Scarborough idea was rejected out of hand. A decision on the continuance of the Easter trains was to be dependent on the loadings of the 1959 trains, and as these were 324 from London and 291 from Scotland it was recommended that these be kept running. The haemorrhaging of Scotland-originating traffic was however a worrying statistic, and all the usual probable reasons were again put forward for this, including this year's shortening of the season.

Financial Results

From	Trains		Tickets		Receipts
	Out	Rtn	Adult	Child	£
St Pancras	26	28	8,114	1,395	37,449
Marylebone	20	21	4,848	766	22,232
Glasgow	41	42	15,574	1,833	70,302
Edinburgh	25	28	7,107	1,126	33,848
Totals	112	119	35,634	5,120	163,831

Receipts of £6,628 also accrued to the Hotels & Catering Services in supplying refreshments en route. After allowing for all costs, it was estimated that the profit margin of receipts over direct costs for 1959 amounted to £31,259 compared with £40,189 for the 1958 season. Although the reduction in receipts has been continuous since 1954, the traffic was still substantial, showing a higher average receipt per train in 1959 than in any previous year except 1958. No adverse criticism was received regarding the increase of 5s in the adult return fare.

Going South?

TRAVEL BY ★ STARLIGHT SPECIAL ★ TO

LONDON

Outward from Glasgow (St. Enoch) on Friday 27th March and Fridays 15th May to 11th September, 1959, inclusive

- ★ STAY 8 OR 15 DAYS
- ★ EXPRESS NIGHT TRAVEL
- ★ CLEAN, COMFORTABLE CORRIDOR COACHES
- ★ SEAT GUARANTEED
- ★ BUFFET AVAILABLE
- ★ CHILDREN HALF FARE
- ★ ADVANCE BOOKING ESSENTIAL

RETURN **85/-** FARE

SEE SEPARATE HANDBILL FOR FULL DETAILS

Be sure to visit the
SCOTTISH INDUSTRIES EXHIBITION
KELVIN HALL, GLASGOW
3rd to 19th September, 1959

FREEDOM OF SCOTLAND TICKET

A "FREEDOM OF SCOTLAND" Ticket permits seven days unlimited travel between all British Railways (Scottish Region) Stations and also by the Steamer Services of The Caledonian Steam Packet Company Limited between Clyde Coast and Loch Lomond Piers (where service in operation).

FIRST CLASS	RATES	SECOND CLASS
£9		**£6**

Where one and a half or more tickets for one family travelling together for the same seven days are taken out, a reduced rate of £7 10s. (First Class) and £5 (Second Class) will be charged.

Children 3 years of age and under 14 years of age, half rate.

The tickets are issued during the period 1st March to 31st October, 1959.

ASK FOR SPECIAL PROGRAMME GIVING FULL DETAILS

TRAVEL BY DIESEL CAR SERVICES BETWEEN

GLASGOW and EDINBURGH

WITH A

CHEAP DAY RETURN TICKET

From GLASGOW (Central or Queen Street)

TO EDINBURGH

(PRINCES STREET, WAVERLEY or HAYMARKET)

EVERY DAY (INCLUDING SUNDAY), BY ANY TRAIN AT OR AFTER 9.30 a.m.

The tickets are not valid by Pullman Car trains between Glasgow (Queen Street) and Edinburgh (Waverley) in either direction.

NOTE.—On Sundays, the train service is between Glasgow (Queen Street) and Edinburgh (Waverley).

FIRST **12/3** CLASS	RETURN FARES	SECOND **8/2** CLASS

The tickets are valid on the date for which issued and by the services specified

8

An ScR advertisement for the 1959 season, putting 'Starlights' in the context of other promotions current at the time. (BRB Residuary)

The 1960 Season

Advance bookings opened on 1 February and the fare remained at 85s, but the big change was the implementation of the 'single terminus in London' policy mooted at the end of 1958, resulting in all Starlight Specials being concentrated on Marylebone.

Consequently, the season began on Thursday 14 April with the departure of M696 from Marylebone at 10.15 p.m. reaching Waverley at 8.17/8.35 a.m. and St Enoch at 9.55 a.m.; an eleven-coach formation of 363 tons, returning the following day as C607, left St Enoch at 8.0 p.m., reaching Woodford Halse at 5.59 a.m. and Marylebone at 7.38 a.m. From this it will be seen that management's wish to see speedier journey times did not materialise; indeed the run from Glasgow was slower than before – and yet this was the source of the main core traffic.

The following weekend saw the return workings, both seven-coach formations of 231 tons.

Saturday 23 April	213	
St Enoch dep. 7.45 p.m.	Waverley 9.2/9.23 p.m.	Marylebone 7.20 a.m.
Saturday 23 April	M681	
Marylebone dep. 11.10 p.m.	Waverley 9.20/9.30 a.m.	Queen St (HL) 10.50 a.m.

Thereafter there was a break in service until the commencement of weekly outward Starlights on Friday 20 May, the last being on Friday 23 September. (The season was shown as officially ending on 9 September, but the STNs show extra workings on Friday 16th train 215 ex-Edinburgh and Friday 23rd train 213 combined train ex-Glasgow.)

There was also a plan to use new BR standard RMB stock (the first being unveiled to the public on 28 March at Buchanan Street) on Starlight Specials, but it is unlikely that this happened (in 1960 anyway). (RMB: Restaurant Miniature Buffet car). The standard formation was now BSK/4SK/CAF/5SK/BSK formed of twelve coaches of 374 tons.

Note that RCAF has reverted to simply CAF again.

Some details of early season workings are available:

Friday 3 June

C4		215	
from St Enoch & Waverley		St Enoch dep.	8.0 p.m.
to		Waverley	9.26/9.40 p.m.
Nottingham (V)	4.21/4.26 a.m. (W)	Nottingham (V)	4.41/4.47 a.m. (W)
Leicester (C)	4.54/4.56 a.m. (L)	Leicester (C)	5.15/5.16 a.m. (L)
W'ford Halse	5.39 a.m.	W'ford Halse	5.59 a.m.
Marylebone	7.25 a.m. (Saturday)	Marylebone	7.40 a.m.

Note: five or six minutes for a water stop is possible, but one or two minutes for a loco change is impracticable! Perhaps this Leicester stop indicated 'crew change' only, with engine working through to/from Darnall (Sheffield)?

Friday 10 June

M695		M696	
Marylebone dep. 9.45 p.m.		M'bone dep.	10.15 p.m.
Leicester (C)	12.9/12.10 a.m. (L)	Leicester (C)	12.49/12.50 a.m. (L)
Nottingham (V)	12.38/12.44 a.m. (W)	Nottingham (V)	1.8/1.24 a.m. (W)
Waverley	8.2 a.m. (Saturday)	St Enoch	9.45 a.m. (Saturday)

Examples of workings to other destinations include:

Friday 8 July

213   Aberdeen 4.40 p.m.   Waverley 8.45/9.23 p.m. Marylebone 7.30 a.m.

Friday 15 July

446   Cardenden 6.35 p.m.   Waverley 8.15/8.35 p.m. Marylebone 6.48 a.m.

Saturday 16 July

M674		M676	
Marylebone dep. 10.10 p.m.		12.1 a.m. (Sun)	
Carlisle	6.48/6.59 a.m.	8.16/8.26 a.m.	
Hawick	8.7/8.13 a.m.	9.34/9.40 a.m.	
Waverley	9.29 a.m.	10.57 a.m.	

Friday 22 July

	446	213	C605	
Dundee	?	?	Galashiels 8.5 p.m.	
Perth	6.28/6.33 p.m.	7.23/7.28 p.m.	Hawick	8.34/8.45 a.m.
Waverley	8.15/8.35 p.m.	9.02/9.23 p.m.	Carlisle	10.1/10.3 p.m.
Marylebone	6.48 a.m.	7.30 a.m.	M'bone	6.25 a.m.

(C605 formation BSK/4SK/CC/4SK/BSK = 363 tons)

Saturday 30 July

M674		M678
Marylebone dep. 10.10 p.m.		12.30 a.m. (Sun)
Dearn Junction	2.51 a.m.	5.19 a.m.
York	3.36/3.45 a.m.	5.55/6.5 a.m.
Newcastle	5.40/5.50 a.m.	8.3/8.13 a.m.
Waverley	8.15/8.35 a.m.	10.39/10.49 a.m.
Kirkcaldy	9.19 a.m.	Cardenden 12.16 p.m.

Formation (both trains): BSO/8SO/CC/BSO, i.e. cafeteria car not central?

Saturday 6 August

M674	M678
Marylebone dep. 10.10 p.m.	12.30 a.m. (Sun)
Carlisle 6.27/6.37 a.m.	8.55/9.4 a.m.
Hawick 7.47/7.53 a.m.	10.18/10.26 a.m.
Waverley 9.12/9.22 a.m.	11.47/12.0 a.m.
Dundee (TB) 10.55 a.m.	1.45 p.m.

The outbound season concluded with the running of a combined train (213, according to the STNs) on:

Friday 23 September
St Enoch departing at 7.45 p.m., reaching Waverley at 9.2/9.23 p.m., Newcastle at 11.44 p.m. and M'bone at 7.20 a.m.

Further 'Starlight Special' details are again available from the following document.

Newcastle Station Workings for Saturday 30 July 1960

215
9.40 p.m. Waverley–Marylebone (Friday 29 July)
arrive 12.3 a.m. depart 12.11 a.m. from platform 9
engine working inbound – LE to Gateshead (G6 dsl)
engine working outbound – LE from Gateshead (G78)

214
9.35 p.m. Marylebone–Waverley (Friday 29 July)
arrive 5.13 a.m. depart 5.22 a.m. from platform 8; 11coaches
engine working inbound – LE to Gateshead (G Add)
engine working outbound – LE to Gateshead (G Add)

216
9.45 p.m. Marylebone–Waverley (Friday 29 July)
arrive 5.21 a.m. depart 5.32 a.m. from platform 9
engine working inbound – LE to Gateshead (G78M)
engine working outbound – 4.49 a.m. ex-King's Cross (G6A dsl)

213
8.35 p.m. Waverley–Marylebone
arrive 11.15 p.m. depart 11.27 p.m. from platform 10
engine working inbound – LE to Gateshead (Sc Add)
engine working outbound – LE from Gateshead (Sc Add)

215
9.5 p.m. Waverley–Marylebone
arrive 11.31 p.m. depart 11.42 p.m. from platform 9
engine working inbound – LE to Gateshead (Sc7)
engine working outbound – LE from Gateshead (G76M)
(BRB Residuary)

Financial Results

From	Trains		Tickets		Receipts
	Out	Rtn	Adult	Child	£
Marylebone	42	43	11,992	1,825	54,844
Glasgow	39	42	13,616	1,776	63,005
Edinburgh	27	27	6,619	1,104	32,450
Totals	108	112	32,227	4,705	150,299
Totals 1959	112	119	35,643	5,120	163,831
Totals 1958	124	131	41,318	5,768	189,989
Totals 1957	165	168	52,768	7,425	228,244
Totals 1956	180	186	59,174	8,150	239,880
Totals 1955	185	189	64,535	8,640	240,994
Totals 1954	196	204	73,793	9,118	274,232
Totals 1953	209	220	67,717	7,811	250,677

After allowing for all costs, the estimated profit margin for 1960 was assessed as £20,918 compared with £31,259 for the 1959 season.

The Hotels & Catering Services recorded additional receipts of £8,708.

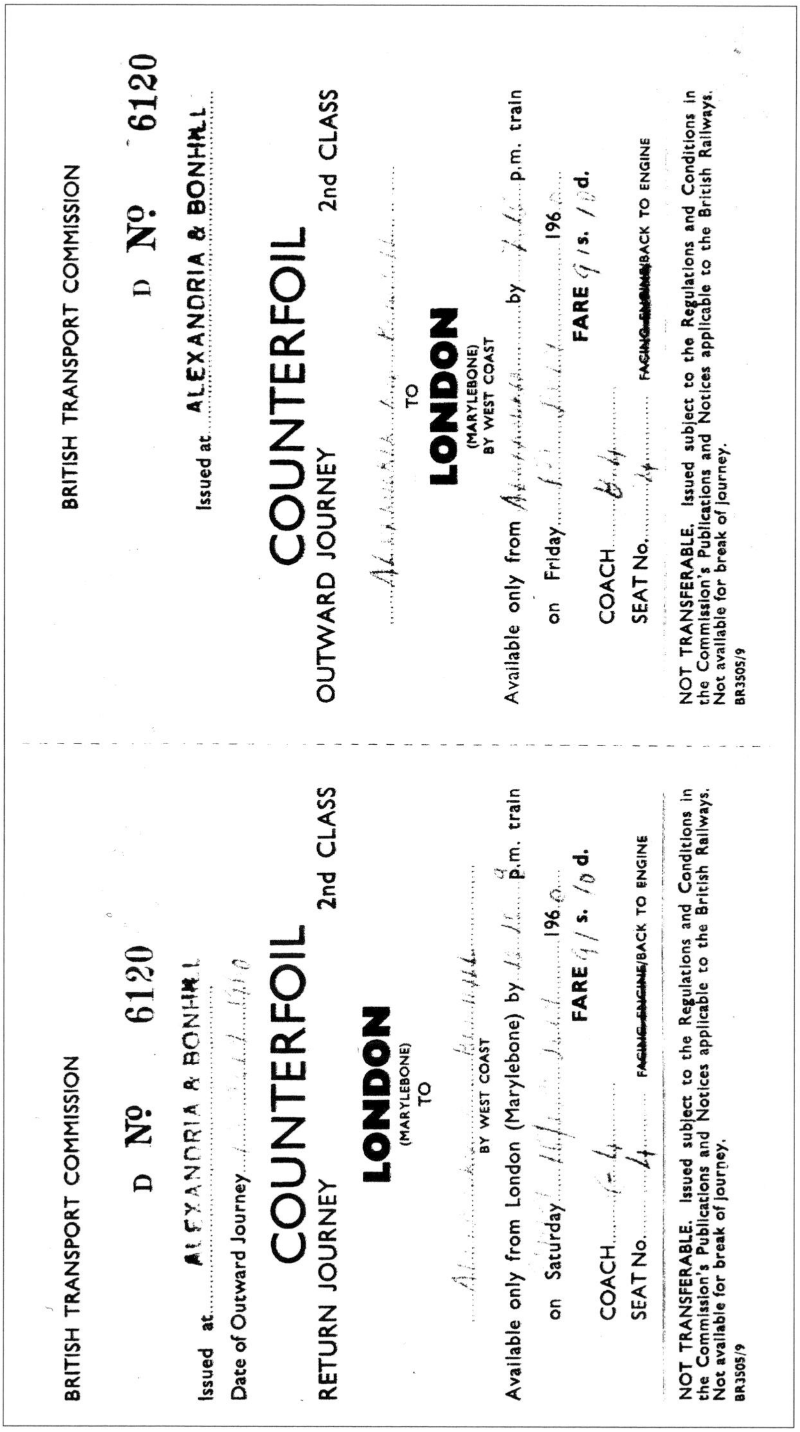

BRITISH TRANSPORT COMMISSION

D Nº 6120

Issued at ALEXANDRIA & BONHILL

Date of Outward Journey

COUNTERFOIL

RETURN JOURNEY 2nd CLASS

LONDON (MARYLEBONE) TO

BY WEST COAST

Available only from London (Marylebone) by p.m. train

on Saturday 196

FARE s. d.

COACH

SEAT No. FACING ENGINE/BACK TO ENGINE

NOT TRANSFERABLE. Issued subject to the Regulations and Conditions in the Commission's Publications and Notices applicable to the British Railways. Not available for break of journey.

BR3505/9

BRITISH TRANSPORT COMMISSION

D Nº 6120

Issued at ALEXANDRIA & BONHILL

COUNTERFOIL

OUTWARD JOURNEY 2nd CLASS

TO

LONDON (MARYLEBONE) BY WEST COAST

Available only from by p.m. train

on Friday 196

FARE s. d.

COACH

SEAT No. FACING ENGINE/BACK TO ENGINE

NOT TRANSFERABLE. Issued subject to the Regulations and Conditions in the Commission's Publications and Notices applicable to the British Railways. Not available for break of journey.

BR3505/9

Counterfoils for both out and back journeys (now 2nd class) from/to a station on the Balloch branch. Note that Marylebone is now the London terminus, and the add-on fare to the 85*s* 'Starlight' price is 6*s* 10*d* return. The holiday was for ten days. (Brian Pask)

Year-on-Year Results:

Year	Originating in England Passengers	Receipts £	Decrease (Increase) Pass	£	Originating in Scotland Passengers	Receipts £	Decrease (Increase) Pass	£
1953	30,266	99,738			45,262	50,939		
1954	31,613	103,206	(1,347)	(3,468)	51,298	171,026	(6,036)	(20,087)
1955	27,124	88,040	4,489	15,166	46,051	152,954	5,247	18,072
1956	25,845	90,077	1,279	(2,037)	41,479	149,880	4,572	3,074
1957	22,765	84,724	3,080	5,353	37,428	143,520	4,051	6,360
1958	16,247	64,007	6,518	20,717	30,839	125,982	6,589	17,598
1959	15,123	59,681	1,124	4,326	25,640	104,150	5,199	21,772
1960	13,817	54,844	1,306	4,837	23,115	95,455	2,525	8,695

For the first time, all Starlight traffic was concentrated on Marylebone as the London terminus, with consequent cost savings. However, the journey times remained excessive, with Edinburgh trains scheduled to take approximately ten hours and ten minutes, and Glasgow trains no less than approximately eleven hours and forty minutes – a considerable slowing for direct services to St Enoch, and not a good selling point! The operating department was therefore again urged to give special attention to the need to improve overall journey times, and punctuality in running, for the next season.

Passenger numbers, and receipts, were again down on the previous year, and once again reduced spending power (especially in Scotland), increased use of private cars for holiday purposes – the landmark BMC Mini had become available from August 1959 – and the growth of Continental holidays were all cited as plausible reasons for this. Regardless of these, it must be said that, for its part, the BTC had hardly made Starlights a more attractive product over the eight years of their operation. The rolling stock was virtually that which began the facility in 1953 (itself of late LNER or LMS designs) while the cafeteria cars were even older – though converted from their original use. Schedules had seen little advance (and the west coast route was now slower still) and there was little prospect of any newer vehicles in either category entering Starlight service. In this respect there had already been a cull of 2,000 older low-capacity loco-hauled stock and a further reduction of 1,500 was already planned to take place before the end of 1961, with more to follow. Clearly non-timetabled train provision was about to be squeezed as never before, and the prospect of rolling stock improvements for these trains was therefore nil.

Observations and workings throughout the season

1. Friday 15 Apr, 60160 *Auld Reekie* heads the first southbound train out of St Enoch for Marylebone, loco working through to Newcastle.
2. Saturday 9 July, 45605 *Cyprus* and 45608 *Gibraltar* (both 55A Leeds Holbeck engines) bring two ex-Glasgow Starlights into Marylebone.
3. Friday 15 July 5.0 p.m. from St Enoch departs behind 40642 + 44898. Friday 15 July 7.45 p.m. from St Enoch departs behind 40645 + 45677 *Beatty*.
4. Saturday 16 July, 45589 *Gwalior* (Holbeck) and 45636 *Uganda* (Leicester) bring two further Starlights into London – possibly the same as those on the 9th.

Starlight Special

London-Edinburgh

Glasgow

90s. return

Including reserved seats

CHILDREN HALF FARE

**Thursday 30th March and Friday nights
from 19th May to 8th September inclusive
1961**

STAY 8 OR 15 DAYS · · · NIGHT TRAVEL

BUFFET AVAILABLE · BOOK IN ADVANCE

★ **STARLIGHT SPECIAL TRAINS**, one class only, will run on Thursday 30th March and Friday nights, 19th May to 8th September inclusive, 1961 from London to Glasgow and London to Edinburgh. Passengers will return by Special trains on Saturday nights the 8th or 15th day after arrival(the 9th or 16th day in the case of passengers departing on 30th March)

★ **STARLIGHT SPECIAL TRAINS** assure seats to all passengers. Accommodation is limited and for this reason it is **essential** that passengers *BOOK IN ADVANCE STATING THE DATE ON WHICH THEY DESIRE TO TRAVEL FORWARD AND RETURN.*

★ **STARLIGHT SPECIAL TRAINS** are available **only** to holders of Starlight Special tickets specifying the appropriate train and date of travel.

★ **STARLIGHT SPECIAL TRAINS** run as shown below, and light refreshments are obtainable.

OUTWARD JOURNEY				RETURN JOURNEY		
FRIDAY NIGHTS (also Thursday 30th March)				**SATURDAY NIGHTS**		
	Combined Trains ¶	Independent Trains †			Combined Trains ¶	Independent Trains †
London Marylebone	dep. 10 15 p.m.	dep. 9 45 p.m.	Glasgow St. Enoch		dep. 7 45 p.m.	dep. 8 00 p.m.
Edinburgh Waverley	arr. 8 21 a.m.	arr. 8 02 a.m.	London Marylebone		arr. —	arr. 7 20 a.m.
London Marylebone	dep. —	dep. 10 15 p.m.	Edinburgh Waverley		dep. 9 23 p.m.	dep. 9 05 p.m.
Glasgow St. Enoch	arr. 9 45 a.m.	arr. 9 45 a.m.	London Marylebone		arr. 7 30 a.m.	arr. 7 05 a.m.

¶—Combined trains to Glasgow and Edinburgh will leave London Marylebone Thursday 30th March and Fridays, 26th May and 8th September. Similarly on Saturdays 8th and 15th April and 23rd September combined trains will run from Glasgow and Edinburgh to Marylebone.

†—Departures on Friday nights 19th May and 2nd June to 1st September inclusive. Return trains Saturday nights 27th May to 16th September inclusive.

★ **STARLIGHT SPECIAL TRAIN TICKETS** are on sale at London Terminal Stations, also at principal suburban stations, Railway Ticket Offices and Ticket Agencies in the London area. Remittances for the fare, **90/-,** which includes a reserved seat in each direction (half fare for children aged 3 but under 14 years) must accompany all postal applications to :

Enquiry Office, Marylebone Station, London, N.W.1.

★ **STARLIGHT SPECIAL TICKETS ARE NOT TRANSFERABLE** and are issued subject to the bye-laws, regulations and conditions contained in the publications and notices of or applicable to the British Transport Commission. They are not available for break of journey. British Railways do not undertake to refund the value of lost, mislaid or unused tickets. Further information may be obtained on application to :

DISTRICT PASSENGER MANAGER, *Euston House, London, N.W.1* (Tel. Euston 7070)

TRAVEL LIGHT — SEND YOUR LUGGAGE IN ADVANCE

For Passengers who prefer a Combined Road/Rail facility to Glasgow or Edinburgh by ordinary services (out by road return by rail or vice versa) tickets are obtainable at a fare of 116/- from Scottish Omnibuses Ltd., 298, Regent Street, London, W.1, who will supply details on request.

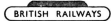

BRITISH RAILWAYS

B.R. 35001   LMR   January 1961   Printed in Great Britain   Stafford & Co., Ltd., Netherfield, Nottingham.

(BRB Residuary)

The 1961 Season

The first outbound departure from London was again on Maundy Thursday (30 March) and this set formed the first Up train from Glasgow and Edinburgh the following day, Good Friday 31 March. The fare was however raised to 90s, which included the seat reservation, now 2s per person.

The split between combined trains (serving both Glasgow and Edinburgh to/from London) and independent trains (St Enoch–Marylebone and Waverley–Marylebone) was designated as on the handbill illustrated. (This is for London-originating traffic and hence does not show Friday departures from Scotland, nor the times of trains returning from Glasgow/Edinburgh on Saturday). The first of these ran on:

Saturday 8 April
Nine-coach load, 279 tons including cafeteria car. 444 left St Enoch at 7.45 p.m. reaching Waverley at 9.2/9.23 p.m. and Marylebone at 7.30 a.m. (Sun).

The first scheduled independent Starlights from Scotland were in fact also run as a combined train, as follows:

Friday 19 May
Eight-coach load, 264 tons inc cafeteria car. 215 departed St Enoch at 8.0 p.m. reaching Waverley at 9.25/9.40 p.m. and Marylebone 7.37 a.m. (Saturday).

The last Down combined train on 26 May was M696 and ran to the advertised timings.

The season of regular weekly Friday night departures began on 19 May, with the summer timetable coming into force on 13 June. From this date BR further extended its usage of four-character train descriptions, the first application to Starlights probably being on:

Friday 30 June
1X56 Waverley 8.35 p.m.   Marylebone 6.55 a.m. (Saturday)   (ten coaches, 330 tons)
1X57 Waverley 9.5 p.m.   Marylebone 7.8 a.m.   (eleven coaches, 363 tons)

Extended services again ran, a sample being re-designated as follows:

Friday 7 July
1M95 departs from Aberdeen at 4.50 p.m., reaching Waverley at 9.25/9.40 p.m. and Marylebone 7.37 a.m. (Saturday).

Friday 14 July
1X56 starts Cardenden 6.40 p.m.
1M95 starts Kirkcaldy 8.39 p.m.

Friday 21 July
1X56 starts Dundee (West) 7.0 p.m.

Saturday 22 July
1S86 departs from Marylebone at 9.50 p.m., reaching Waverley at 8.20/8.35 p.m. and Aberdeen at 12.23 p.m. (Sun).

Friday 28 July
1M99	Galashiels dep.	7.40 p.m.
	Hawick	8.9/8.20 p.m.
	Carlisle	9.36/9.45 p.m.
	Marylebone	6.28 a.m. (Saturday) (9 coaches, 297 tons)

Saturday 29 July
1S85	Marylebone dep. 9.40 p.m. extended to Kirkcaldy 8.28 a.m.
1S86	Marylebone dep. 9.50 p.m. extended to Cardenden 9.33 a.m.

Saturday 12 August
1X49	Marylebone	12.1 a.m. (Sun)
	Carlisle	8.22/8.30 a.m.
	Hawick	9.45/9.53 a.m.
	Galashiels	10.22 a.m. (nine coaches, 297 tons)

At the end of the season, the first Up combined train ran on:

Friday 8 September
1M95 – running to the timings of 215 on 19 May (but eleven coaches, 363 tons), and the final Up working:

Saturday 23 September
1X47 – running to the timings of 444 on 8 April

Within this four-character system:

1   indicated express passenger

M   indicated Inter-Regional train with a London Midland Region destination

S   indicated Inter-Regional train with a Scottish Region destination

X   indicated Inter-Regional train with an excursion or special passenger train.

In addition to the above, there were two departures scheduled on Fridays from Marylebone to St Enoch at 10.15 p.m. (until 1 September inc.) and 11.0 p.m. (14 July to 18 August inc.) and on Saturday at 11.10 p.m. plus 11.30 p.m. (15 July to 12 August and 26 August; 5 Aug going to Galashiels).

Two up services left St Enoch for Marylebone on both Fridays and Saturday; 8.0 p.m. Friday (until 1 September inc.), 8.0 p.m. Saturday, 8.20 p.m. Friday (30 June to 11 August inc.) and 8.20 p.m. Saturday (22 July to 2 September inc.).

The standard formation was the same as that for 1960.

Observations and workings throughout the season

1. Friday 31 Mar, 60824 heads first Up combined train out of St Enoch at 8.0 p.m. Stock included what the press advertisement had called a 'Modern Buffet Car' but turned out to be converted kitchen car M30001M.
2. Saturday 8 July, 70053 *Moray Firth* (55A Holbeck) brings a Starlight from St Enoch into Marylebone, and 60893 (34E Neasden) brings in another, from Waverley.

Friday 14 July. 45384 + 45720 *Indomitable* work past Bellahouston on the 8.0 p.m. 'Starlight' carrying a four-character reporting number on the second loco 1M8x. (J. L. Stevenson)

3. Friday 14 July, some of the Glasgow Fair traffic leaves St Enoch as follows:
   44900 + 46130 *The West Yorkshire Regiment* on the 5 p.m.
   45590 *Travancore* + 45621 *Northern Rhodesia* on the 7.45 p.m.
   45384 + 45720 *Indomitable* on the 8.0 p.m.
4. Saturday 22 July, 60052 *Prince Palatine* heads a Down working between York and Newcastle.
5. Saturday 5 Aug, 70044 *Earl Haig* enters Marylebone, having worked through from Leeds.
6. Saturday 19 Aug, 70054 *Dornoch Firth* does the same as 70044.
7. Friday 8 Sept, D8076 and D8081 depart St Enoch on the combined Up train, 1M95, at 8.0 p.m. (NB this is the first known *identifiable* use of diesels on these trains.)

Financial Results

From	Trains		Tickets		Receipts £
	Out	Rtn	Adult	Child	
Marylebone	38	43	10,733	1,450	50,400
Glasgow	34	34	11,563	1,440	55,737
Edinburgh	27	27	6,118	1,014	31,294
Totals	99	104	28,387	3,904	137,431

An amount of £7,681 accrued to the Hotels & Catering Services through the supply of refreshments on trains.

During the 1961 season, seventeen fewer trains were run than in 1960 and bookings were lower by 12 per cent from Marylebone, 16 per cent from Glasgow and 8 per cent from Edinburgh. Carryings were affected to some extent by the reduction in the number of trains – particularly at the peak weekends immediately preceding the Scottish City Trade Holidays, when the rolling stock resources available were insufficient to cater for the full demands.

However, the direct costs of running these trains, now reassessed on a current day (1961) basis, revealed that the estimated margin of receipts over direct costs was £54,131 – equivalent to approximately 40 per cent of receipts. These are still substantial, and in view of the margin of profit, it was considered that it would be a retrograde step either to withdraw the excursions or to make a material change in their presentation to the public. It was also the opinion that, while coaching stock resources would be less in 1962, on balance better utilisation of stock and more remunerative working was likely if Starlight Specials continued, on the understanding that the number of trains scheduled on any occasion did not exceed the number actually run in 1961. The operating committee again recorded in their minutes that every endeavour would continue to be made to accelerate the running times and to maintain punctuality of these trains.

Bookings and revenue at Easter 1961 were indicative of a demand at this holiday period that should be met, and it was considered that net revenue would benefit from the running of one combined train both from London and Scotland, with the return train scheduled for the following week.

The Starlight facility had again held its own against road competition and encouraged travel to more distant resorts. The express bus fare was increased from 90s to 100s from 14 August 1961 and as Starlight fares had always approximated to the competitive bus fare, a similar increase was thought appropriate for the 1962 Starlight season.

However, on 1 April 1961 the State-owned (and State-subsidised) domestic airline BEA (British European Airways) began operating turbo-prop 'Vanguard' aeroplanes on their London–Glasgow route. BEA were making five round trips per day offering 10,500 passenger seats each week, with off-peak tourist class fares as low as 83s one way, and airfield-to-airfield timings of 85 minutes. For the first time in Great Britain, air travel became a real competitor in the domestic market not only for first class but also second class rail travel, and of course for holiday travel as well. Couple this threat to Anglo-Scottish rail journeys with a road-coach industry that was gearing up for an ever-increasing mileage of motorways that promised to cut their timings attractively, and BR's hold on long-distance services, holiday or otherwise, looked likely to weaken.

GLASGOW or **EDINBURGH** *to* **LONDON**

EXPRESS NIGHT TRAVEL

STAY 8 or 15 DAYS

RESERVED SEATS

BUFFET

£5

Second Class
Return Fare

by

Starlight Special

BRITISH RAILWAYS

BOOK NOW

Friday 20th April & Fridays 1st June to 7th Sept. 1962

FOR FULL DETAILS SEE OTHER SIDE

★ **STARLIGHT SPECIAL TRAINS,** one class only, will run on Friday nights 20th April and 1st June to 7th September, 1962, inclusive, from Glasgow to London and Edinburgh to London. Passengers will return by special trains from London on Saturday nights the eighth or fifteenth day after arrival.

★ **STARLIGHT SPECIAL TRAINS** assure seats to all passengers. Accommodation is limited and for this reason it is essential that passengers *BOOK IN ADVANCE STATING THE DATE ON WHICH THEY DESIRE TO TRAVEL FORWARD AND RETURN.*

★ **STARLIGHT SPECIAL TRAINS** are available only to holders of Starlight Special Tickets specifying the appropriate train and date of travel.

★ **STARLIGHT SPECIAL TRAINS** run as shown below, and light refreshments are obtainable.

OUTWARD JOURNEY—FRIDAY NIGHTS

	20th April and 7th September	1st June to 31st August	1st June to 31st August
	p.m.	p.m.	p.m.
GLASGOW (St. Enoch) ....leave	8 0	8 0	—
EDINBURGH (Waverley) ...... ,,	9 23	—	9 23
	a.m.	a.m.	a.m.
LONDON (Marylebone)........arrive	7 25	7A 20	B

RETURN JOURNEY—SATURDAY NIGHTS

	28th April, 5th May 15th and 22nd September	9th June to 8th September	9th June to 8th September
	p.m.	p.m.	p.m.
LONDON (Marylebone)........leave	11* 30	11 25	9 55
	a.m.		a.m.
EDINBURGH (Waverley) ......arrive	—	—	7C 40
EDINBURGH (Princes St.)...... ,,	10D 15	—	—
GLASGOW (St. Enoch) .... ,,	—	10 25	—
GLASGOW (Central) .... ,,	10 20	—	—

A—On mornings of 30th June, 14th and 28th July, arrives Marylebone 7.25 a.m.

B—On mornings of 2nd, 9th and 16th June, arrives Marylebone 7.20 a.m. On mornings of 23rd June, 21st July, 11th, 18th and 25th August and 1st September, arrives Marylebone 6.45 a.m. On mornings of 30th June and 7th July, arrives Marylebone 7.30 a.m. On mornings of 14th and 28th July and 4th August, arrives Marylebone 6.55 a.m.

C—On mornings of 15th, 22nd and 29th July, arrives Edinburgh (Waverley) 7.55 a.m.

D—Change Carstairs.

*—On Saturdays, 5th May and 22nd September, Glasgow passengers return by 9.25 p.m. ordinary train from London (St. Pancras) to Glasgow (St. Enoch) and Edinburgh passengers return by 9.10 p.m. ordinary train from London (St. Pancras) to Edinburgh (Waverley):

★ **STARLIGHT SPECIAL TRAIN TICKETS** are on sale as shown below and at principal suburban stations and at Railway Ticket Agents in the Glasgow and Edinburgh areas. Remittances for the fare 100/- which includes a reserved seat in each direction (half fare for children aged 3 but under 14 years) must accompany all postal applications to:—

FOR BOOKINGS FROM GLASGOW:	**FOR BOOKINGS FROM EDINBURGH:**
Starlight Enquiry Office,	Starlight Enquiry Office,
St. Enoch Station,	Waverley Station,
Glasgow.	Edinburgh.
Telephone No.: CITy 6128.	Telephone No.: WAVerley 2477. (Extension 444-5)

★ **STARLIGHT SPECIAL TICKETS ARE NOT TRANSFERABLE** and are issued subject to the bye-laws, regulations and conditions contained in the publications and notices of or applicable to the British Transport Commission. They are not available for break of journey. British Railways do not undertake to refund the value of lost, mislaid or unused tickets. Further information may be obtained on application to:

DISTRICT PASSENGER MANAGER, 87 Union Street, Glasgow, C.1.

DISTRICT COMMERCIAL MANAGER, 23 Waterloo Place, Edinburgh.

TRAVEL LIGHT—SEND YOUR LUGGAGE IN ADVANCE

For passengers who prefer a Combined Road/Rail facility to London by ordinary services (out by road, return by rail or vice versa) tickets are obtainable at a fare of £6 1 0 from Scottish Omnibuses Ltd. 290 Buchanan Street, Glasgow, or 45 Princes Street, Edinburgh, who will supply details on request.

B.R. 35001—MS—February, 1962—B 33037   McCorquodale, Glasgow.

The 1962 Season

For this year the fare was again raised, this time to £5 return, and the main season shortened slightly, beginning on Friday 1 June and ending on Friday 7 September. Bookings opened on 1 February, and the Easter trains ran as follows:

Thursday 19 April			*Friday 20 April*		
1X87	Marylebone dep.	10.20 p.m.	1M95	St Enoch dep.	8.10 p.m.
	Newcastle	5.59 a.m.		Waverley	9.25/9.40 p.m.
	Waverley	8.16/8.34 a.m.		Newcastle	11.57 p.m.
	St Enoch	9.40 a.m. (Fri)		Marylebone	7.20 a.m. (Saturday)
(twelve coaches, 396 tons)			(ten coaches, 330 tons)		

These were returned as usual: nine or sixteen days later for the 19 April departures, and eight or fifteen days later for the southbound train. The first return working was therefore on:

Saturday 28 April			
	1X47	St Enoch dep.	7.45 p.m.
		Waverley	9.2/9.23 p.m.
		Newcastle	11.48 p.m.
(nine coaches, 279 tons)		Marylebone	7.35 a.m. (Sun)

As none of these timings correspond exactly to those on the handbill (Scottish issue), which in any case gives only timings for the 'parent' trains, it is perhaps instructive to examine this season's illustrated schedules (as per handbill) more closely.

Despite repeated Management pleas for the journey times to be accelerated, it will be seen that:

Northbound   fastest time to Edinburgh was nine hours and forty-five minutes (1953 nine hours and thirty-seven minutes)
slowest time to Edinburgh was ten and three quarter hours, to Princes Street, with a change at Carstairs!
fastest time to Glasgow was ten hours and fifty minutes, to Central (1953 ten hours and thirty-five minutes)
slowest time to Glasgow was eleven hours

Southbound quickest time from Edinburgh was nine hours and twenty-two minutes (1953 nine hours ten minutes)
slowest time from Edinburgh was ten hours and seven minutes
quickest time from Glasgow was eleven hours and twenty minutes
(1953 ten hours and twenty-five minutes)
slowest time from Glasgow was eleven hours and twenty-five minutes.

The footnotes to the advertised timings were also more extensive than previously, and for the first time passengers were *instructed* to make a return journey by ordinary train (as opposed to this being an emergency measure) on two dates. As noted above, and also for the first time, returning passengers were to *change* at Carstairs on four dates in order to reach Princes Street – itself a new terminus! The extreme slowness of the Glasgow trains (from whence most patronage derived) was yet again a disappointment.

The main season for Edinburgh traffic commenced on June 1 with the running of 1M94, departing from Waverley at 9.23 p.m., reaching Newcastle at 11.48 p.m. and Marylebone at 7.20 a.m., this being the 'parent' train for southbound east coast Starlights. The first northbound equivalent was on Friday 8 June, timings being 1S86 departing from Marylebone at 9.45 p.m., reaching Newcastle at 5.24 a.m. and Waverley at 8.01 a.m., and the last excursion of the season returned on Saturday 22 September, running into Marylebone as 1X47 (timings above) early on Sunday morning. In between, the various east coast trains ran under the descriptions:

Up Starlights	1M94/95	1M83/87	1X47/50/57
Down Starlights	1S85/86/87	1S50/60	1X49

and a representative sample of these workings are as follows:

Friday 6 July   1X57   *Friday 13 July*
Aberdeen dep. 4.50 p.m.   1M87 Cardenden 6.32 p.m.   M'bone 6.5 a.m.
Dundee   6.33/6.41 p.m.   1M95 Kirkcaldy 8.39 p.m.   M'bone 7.50 a.m.
Thornton Jct 7.33/7.40 p.m. (W)
Marylebone   6.55 a.m. (Saturday)

Saturday 14 July

1S50	Marylebone	8.45 p.m.	Waverley	6.48 a.m.
1S60		9.20 p.m.		7.10 a.m.
1S85		9.45 p.m.		7.40 a.m.
1S86		9.55 p.m.		7.55 a.m.

Friday 20 July

1M87	Dundee (West)	5.35 p.m.	1M95	Dundee (West)	7.0 p.m.
	Perth	6.13 p.m. (L)		Perth	7.36 p.m.
	Waverley	7.43/7.56 p.m.		Dun'line Lower	8.41/8.48 p.m. (W)
	Newcastle	10.22 p.m.		Waverley	9.25/9.40 p.m.
	Marylebone	6.5 a.m.		Newcastle	12.12 a.m.
				Marylebone	7.50 a.m.

(1M87 eight coaches, 264 tons)   (1M95 eleven coaches, 363 tons)

Saturday 21 July

1S85   Marylebone 9.45 p.m.   Aberdeen 9.28 a.m. (Sun)

Friday 27 July

1X50   Galashiels 7.40 p.m.   Hawick 8.9/8.17 p.m.
Carlisle 9.28/9.36 p.m. (L)
M'bone 6.5 a.m. (11 coaches, 363 tons)

Saturday 30 June. Bearing reporting number 1M93, 45659 *Drake* brings the Balloch–Marylebone through East Leake station at 6.42, running late. (David Holmes)

Friday 13 July. 70052 *Firth of Tay* (transferred to Corkerhill in March) powers 1M92, the 8.0 p.m. from St Enoch past the (gas-lit) Paisley Canal line station at Shields Road. (This station closed on 14 February 1966.) On this, the final Glasgow Fair Friday on which Starlights ran, four left St Enoch, plus a further two the next day. (W. A. C. Smith/Transport Treasury)

Saturday 28 July

1S50	Marylebone 8.45 p.m.	Waverley 6.48/7.0 a.m.	Cardenden 8.15 a.m. (Sun)	
1S60	9.20 p.m.	7.10 a.m.		
1S85	9.45 p.m.	7.40/7.52 a.m.	Kirkcaldy 8.38 a.m.	
1S86	9.55 p.m.	7.55 a.m.		

Saturday 4 August

1S50	Marylebone	8.45 p.m.	1S60	Marylebone	9.20 p.m.
	Dearne Jct	1.36 a.m.		Dearne Jct	1.58 a.m.
	Waverley	6.48/7.0 a.m.		Waverley	7.10/7.38 a.m.
	Dundee (Tay Bridge) 8.33 a.m.			Dundee (Tay Bridge) 9.24 a.m.	
(BSK/4SK/CC/4SK/BSK = 363t)			(BSO/3SO/CC/2SO/BSO = 264t)		

Saturday 11 August

1X49	Marylebone	12.1 a.m. (Sun)
	Carlisle	8.25/8.33 a.m. (L)
	Hawick	9.46/9.54 a.m.
	Galashiels	10.23 a.m.

Saturday 22 September

1X47	St Enoch	7.45 p.m.
	Waverley	9.2/9.23 p.m.
	Newcastle	11.48 p.m.
	M'bone	7.30 a.m.

For this season, only one train was timetabled each way from Marylebone to Glasgow (via Carlisle) and vice versa, on both Friday and Saturday nights.

Observations and workings throughout the season

1. Friday 20 Apr, 60802 heads the 8.10 p.m. combined train out of St Enoch.
2. Saturday 9 June, 45690 *Leander* (82E Bristol Barrow Road!) works into Marylebone with a Starlight from Glasgow.
3. Sunday 10 June, 46138 *The London Irish Rifleman* (6J Holyhead shedplate – but recently transferred to 15E Leicester) arrives in M'bone on another Glasgow Starlight.
4. Friday/Saturday 15/16 June, 44936 (2E Saltley) on a Starlight Leicester–York. 46138 (above) on another, again Leicester–York.
5. Friday 29 June Starlight starts from Inverclyde.
6. Friday/Saturday 29/30 June, 60099 *Call Boy* works Waverley–N'castle relieved by 60001 *Sir Ronald Matthews*, from Newcastle to York.
7. Saturday 30 June, 45659 *Drake* heads the Balloch–Marylebone at East Leake.
8. Sunday 1 July, 45677 *Beatty* passes Crookston (on the Paisley Canal Line) with a Down train for St Enoch.
9. Friday 13 July 7.5 p.m. from Coatbridge (Central) via Hamilton and Langside Jct sets off behind 45083 + 45009. 7.45 p.m. from St Enoch via Barrhead leaves behind 44992 + 46117 *Welsh Guardsman*. 8.0 p.m. from St Enoch via Paisley (Canal) is powered by 70052 *Firth of Tay*. 8.20 p.m. 70050 *Firth of Clyde* departs St Enoch running via Paisley (Gilmour Street) on 1M92.
10. Saturday 21 July, 60871 heads 1M95 (7.0 p.m. ex-Dundee) into M'bone.
11. Saturday 11 Aug, 60155 *Borderer* is in charge of a Starlight between Waverley and Newcastle.

Financial Resume 1962 and previous seasons

Year	Trains		Tickets		Receipts
	Out	Rtn	Adult	Child	£
1962	82	91	19,931	2,742	107,616
1961	99	104	28,387	3,904	137,431
1960	108	112	32,227	4,705	150,299
1959	112	119	35,643	5,120	163,831
1958	124	131	41,318	5,768	189,989
1957	165	168	52,768	7,425	228,244
1956	180	186	59,174	8,150	239,880
1955	185	189	64,535	8,640	240,994
1954	196	204	73,793	9,118	274,232
1953	209	220	67,717	7,811	250,677

The continuing decline in patronage was attributable to various changes in circumstances since the introduction of the facility, and it appeared unlikely that the trend would alter in the future. Moreover, the Starlight arrangement made costly demands on rolling stock as little use could be made of the vehicles other than the outward and return weekly journeys, and this problem would be compounded in 1963 by the further contraction of the coaching fleet.

At the outset the rail fare was higher than that charged by bus operators in view of the superiority of the rail service, but in later years the same fare as by road (£5 in 1962) was charged. The regular bus services between London and Glasgow/Edinburgh were now wholly in the hands of BTC operators.

Estimated costs of the 'Starlight Special' trains for 1962 had been calculated and, set against bookings in relation to the present fare of £5, the revenue fell below the total costs incurred.

While Starlight Specials excursions had served a useful purpose in the past, the conclusion was reached, after taking all the facts into consideration, that these trains were no longer an economic proposition and it was therefore agreed that they should be discontinued in their present form in 1963. The traffic conference felt, however, that there was a field for securing additional revenue from the utilisation of marginal stock (if any), and the commercial committee were asked to consider the prospects of introducing reduced fares between England and Scotland by services operating at times when stock would otherwise be idle.

Despite this being a 1956 photo (see the 75/- fare on the Starlight poster) it seems fitting to include it here, as Glasgow's trams stopped running within a few days of the last Starlight Special. Both were terminated in 1962, never to run again. (W. D. McMillar/J. L. Stevenson Collection)

Summary of Significant Yearly Changes

1953: Fare 70s. Only season in which both routes used exclusively compartment stock.

1954: East coast route introduces 'open' stock on all its Starlights.

1955: ASLEF strike 28 May–11 June disrupts programme. East coast reverts to using compartment stock for first two excursions (only) on any one night.

Some Glasgow Fair trains that could not be accommodated on Friday evening set off from Glasgow on Saturday.

1956: Fare 75s. Post-Easter pre-Whitsuntide period sees combined trains from Glasgow/Edinburgh, bringing LNER Pacifics to St Enoch on a scheduled basis for the first time. BR Mk1 catering vehicles (RBs) used for first time?

1957: Fare 80s. As 1956 but latter part of season poorly patronised.

1958: Fare 85s. ScR introduces system of deferred payments. Number of early season specials cancelled. Three Glasgow Fair excursions begin their outward journeys on Saturday – first time this day used for outbound traffic since 1955.

1959: Introduction of break between Easter and Whit holidays. Season also terminates one week earlier; last train uses Buchanan Street – another first.

New hygiene regulations cause catering staff to refuse to work in BSKs, but are persuaded otherwise! Two month national printing strike causes 'loss' of records for much of the season.

1960: Marylebone becomes the sole terminus for Starlight traffic, with consequent slowing of Glasgow trains. First evidence of use of diesel locos over part of the route.

1961: Fare 90s. 4-character train descriptions now used on these trains. First *identifiable* diesels used.

1962: Fare £5. On four dates returning passengers are to change at Carstairs to reach Edinburgh (Princes Street!) – both retrograde firsts. Facility now deemed uneconomic and withdrawn at end of season.

Postscript

The following is extracted from the March 1963 issue of *Modern Railways*, in the 'News and Comment' section:

No more Starlight Specials

There will be no more Starlight Specials between London and Scotland this summer. But the abandonment of this post-war development in cheap travel at weekends, largely over secondary Anglo-Scottish routes and with reduced amenities by comparison with regular services, may well be only the most conspicuous evidence of a general trend in BR passenger train policy this summer. The economics of providing limitless extra and relief trains purely for the summer peaks have been under close scrutiny; fewer Saturday and Sunday additional trains are to be expected this year and the summer timetables will probably show a substantial increase in precisely dated trains. The chief consideration influencing this trend, of course, is the amount of stock that has to be maintained for most of the year without gainful employment for service only at a few peak weekends. When the 'Starlight Special' balance sheet is examined in this light, we are told, the profit margin of these trains is slashed to very small dimensions. BR spokesmen also make the point that they are able to secure satisfactory loadings for the regular Anglo-Scottish services on full and mid-week return fares. The force of the BR argument is obvious in principle, but we would like to be sure that this problem is being reviewed on an all-line basis, and that the predicted summer cuts are not merely the outcome of an arbitrary instruction to the Regions to effect an independent reduction of their rolling stock requirements to a certain level, or to study their own carriage utilisation in isolation. One feels that an all-line survey of all periodical special train demands for local holidays, sporting events, exhibitions, conferences, seaside illuminations and so on might produce a pattern of reasonably continuous employment spread over a good part of each year that would justify the provision of a carefully controlled pool of stock to cover at least a selected proportion of likely special workings in all Regions. The first step would be to agree those periodical trains whose retention would promise the most profit and which were considered particularly desirable from a Public Relations or traffic promotion angle, and then see how far it was possible to roster the necessary stock for these to other likely special work, in any part of the country for the rest of the year.

We regard the abandonment of the Starlight Specials as extremely unfortunate, assuming that the trains' profitability could have been enhanced by a rolling stock scheme such as we have outlined. The Starlights probably attracted many customers who would otherwise not have gone near the railway for a long-distance journey, and some who might have been influenced to try regular services as well. These people will not understand the economics of rolling stock utilisation which have killed the trains and may incline to the suspicion that BR has become disinterested in encouraging new long-distance travellers. To the general public, recollecting both the amount and the type of publicity put out for the Starlight Specials in their heyday, and also the use made of the Starlight fare as a propaganda counter-blast to BEA cut-price travel offers, this abandonment may look like an abject surrender to competition.

(courtesy of Key Publishing Ltd)

AN ALL-IN HOLIDAY WEEK

IN SCOTLAND

FROM

£17 - 4 - 6

CHILDREN UNDER 14 ACCOMPANYING ADULTS £13 - 9 - 6

inclusive of

TRAVEL TICKETS: GUARANTEED SEAT ON TRAINS: ACCOMMODATION: SIGHTSEEING TRIPS: MEALS ON TRAINS: GRATUITIES

from

NEWCASTLE · GATESHEAD · TYNEMOUTH
MORPETH · HEXHAM · DURHAM
SUNDERLAND · SOUTH SHIELDS
and neighbouring towns

EACH SATURDAY from 31st May to 6th September 1958
returning the following Saturday

(Longer periods can be arranged)

Organised by the Creative Tourist Agents Conference in conjunction with British Railways

For further information and booking form with conditions of issue, please enquire at British Railways Stations and Offices, or official railway agents

Another summer-only holiday train - though within Scotland - is illustrated here; this was popular throughout the 1950s with people wanting an attractive tour by rail. (BRB Residuary)

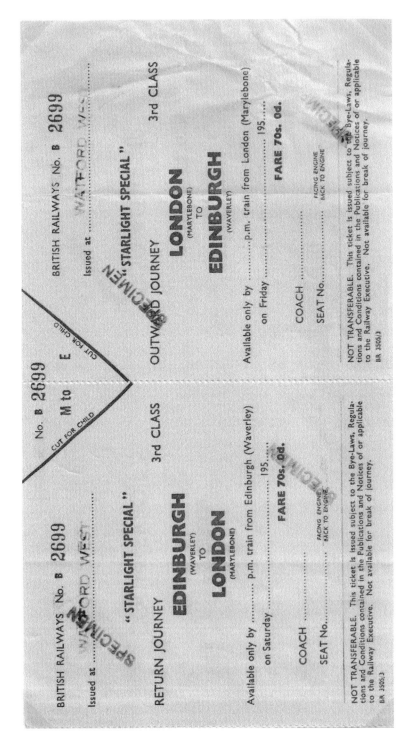

Enlargement of specimen ticket for the East Coast route, held at Watford West; undated but must be for 1953, as 'Railway Executive' is quoted. 'Starlight' tickets were of paper, not the Edmondson card type then in general use.

BRITISH RAILWAYS No. B 5199
WATFORD WEST

Issued at ....

"STARLIGHT SPECIAL"

OUTWARD JOURNEY   3rd CLASS

LONDON
(ST. PANCRAS)
TO
GLASGOW
(ST. ENOCH)

Available only by .... p.m. train from London (St. Pancras)

on Friday .... 195....

FARE 70s. 0d.

COACH ....

SEAT No. ....

FACING ENGINE
BACK TO ENGINE

SPECIMEN

NOT TRANSFERABLE. This ticket is issued subject to the Bye-Laws, Regulations and Conditions contained in the Publications and Notices of or applicable to the Railway Executive. Not available for break of journey.
BR 3505/1

No. B 5199
St. P to   G
CUT FOR CHILD

BRITISH RAILWAYS No. B 5199
WATFORD WEST

Issued at ....

"STARLIGHT SPECIAL"

RETURN JOURNEY   3rd CLASS

GLASGOW
(ST. ENOCH)
TO
LONDON
(ST. PANCRAS)

Available only by .... p.m. train from Glasgow (St. Enoch)

on Saturday .... 195....

FARE 70s. 0d.

COACH ....

SEAT No. ....

FACING ENGINE
BACK TO ENGINE

SPECIMEN

NOT TRANSFERABLE. This ticket is issued subject to the Bye-Laws, Regulations and Conditions contained in the Publications and Notices of or applicable to the Railway Executive. Not available for break of journey.
BR 3505/1

Another enlarged specimen ticket, again 1953, this time for the West Coast route. Note '3rd Class' and the method of identifying a child ticket.